Concentration Mechanism of Tennis, Golf, Soccer, Baseball, and Skiing

Concentration Mechanism of Tennis, Golf, Soccer, Baseball, and Skiing

Benjamin J. An, DDS

Library of Congress Control Number: 2015917538
ISBN: Hardcover   978-1-5144-1958-8
                   Softcover   978-1-5144-1957-1
                   eBook   978-1-5144-1956-4

To order additional copies of this book, contact:
Xlibris
1-888-795-4274
www.Xlibris.com
Orders@Xlibris.com
714210

CONTENTS

Prologue

Sports are specific regulated physical activities. These physical activities are classified as athletic actions. The most common athletic actions are catching, hitting, throwing, and kicking. The basic supporting components of these actions are running and jumping. Many sports were invented by using these physical actions in either individual or group competitions. In baseball games, pitchers throw, batters hit, catchers catch, and fielders catch and throw. These actions are clearly defined. In tennis, a player runs to get to the ball; it is like a catching action. Instead of catching with his hand, he swings with his racket and he makes a hit. The ball flies to a specific distance, clearly just like an action of throw. The mixed nature of catching, hitting, and throwing make up the basic mental problems in the human mind. In soccer games, players run and kick. If you just kick as far as you can, it is a simple kicking action. If you want to kick a specific distance, you introduce specific mental parameters.

The athletic actions in different sports are somewhat different biomechanically; however, they are all identical mentally. Biomechanical skills are very easy to learn. All people need to do is imitate and repeat. All the physical movements are part of human nature. They are born with them. Everyone has his/her own potential and physical limitation to perform these actions. Everyone knows how to hit a ball, but there are good hitters and poor hitters. Everyone can catch a flying ball; some people catch better than others. Everyone knows how to throw a ball; there are, however, good throwers and bad throwers. Everyone can run; some people run faster than others. Through repetition and practice, everyone can get better, and eventually, everyone can reach his/her own physical potential.

Besides the physicality of performing the physical skills, every action requires specific mental parameters to accomplish a desired action. These mental parameters are specific for each athletic action. These mental parameters include what is on your mind (what you are thinking) when you perform that action, what you need to see and the best way to see it, what you need to hear during your action, how you feel, what you want to do and how you do it, and last and the most important, the relationship between your eyes and your thoughts.

It sounds so complicated, but it is not. Though the mental parameters are many, the proper mental parameter each athletic action needs is limited. For the hand sport concerned, the parameters are usually limited to (1) what you think, (2) how you see, and (3) what and how you do. Many of these factors are all related and packed together with one swing movement. This swing movement is a simple swing of your arm or your leg.

The most important part of the mental game is to understand the nature of the mental parameters and use the critically related parameters for each athletic action during execution. Some people may say, "I do not think. I just play." Actually, "I just play" is a thought. If you know the best way to play and to think, just playing will be the perfect thought. If you just want to play hard to win, you may not win. If you just want to play safe to win, you may not be safe to win. Understanding all these mental parameters and not allowing any one of these parameters to interfere with the smooth physical movement of the specific athletic actions is the essence to understanding the meaning of concentration.

When any physical action is applied in a game, it usually induces many environmental interference factors. These factors could be biomechanical, mental, psychological, or just intellectual. Here, I have to say a few words about the intellectual interference because you probably never heard about this term before. It is simply the term I used to describe how our intellectual ability interferes with what we are doing.

We are human. We are born with very strong concept of throwing in our mind. It is an important part of our neurological system. Whenever we do something related to distance, the throwing concept comes in our mind. The concepts of throwing and hitting are related to how we think and how we see with our eyes. The mixed feeling of hitting a tennis ball and where the ball is going creates a tremendous mental problem in sport performance. This is the reason I suggested the term *intellectual interference*.

Proper management of these interference factors is one of the most important challenges among all tennis and golf coaches. It is difficult, because it is the general way we think intellectually. This is a process of concentrating. Very often, we have to stress to a player and ask him to just hit the ball and never worry where the ball is going. The reasoning is, if he hits properly, the ball will go automatically to the place he planned.

A golf stroke is just a swing. You often see a golfer practice his/her swing and aim at some spot or a piece of grass and he swings beautifully every time. However, when he put the little white ball on the ground to hit, the swing changes. When he sees the ball, he also sees where he wants the ball to go or what he wants to do to the ball. The presence of the ball interferes with his thought of how he feels his proper swing. The thing one sees may interfere with what one wants to do. The most important part of the mental game is that the proper mental thought should always be on the action itself.

You have to use your eyes perfectly in order to be a top tennis player. If you see things too hard, it will interfere with what you do. You can overuse your eyes; you can also underuse your eyes. These are all mental problems.

You can watch the golf ball clearly and swing a good golf swing. You can also be a blind person and hit a hole in one. There is a mental difference and a clear explanation.

What enters the player's eyes will give the player something to think about. Whatever the player is thinking may or may not interfere with the player's swing. There is a clear mental explanation for players to follow.

The player may think about what he wants to do with the ball, or he could think what he wants to do without the ball. There is a great difference between the two different ways of thinking. One way of thinking may be much better than the other. There should be much better mental understanding.

Changing of thought is often associated with changing the use of the eyes. Proper use of the eyes and knowing how to control the eye movements are the most critical parts of athletic performance.

A tight end in a football team catches the ball beautifully in practice. However, during football games, he often drops the catch when he thinks about running with the ball too early. Remember, whatever you do, the concentration should always be on the first action.

Tennis is another game that frustrates so many people. A tennis player performs more athletic actions in the shortest time span than in most other sports. When a tennis player runs to the ball, he is performing a catching action. This is what tennis coaches call this—the footwork. Once he gets there, instead of grabbing, he makes a swing. He, then, is performing a hitting action. When the ball is flying over the net and lands within the boundary of the other side of the court, his job is done.

Now let's examine the nature of the actions that the tennis player has done. To rush to the ball while running is a catching action. His swing to make contact with the ball is a hitting action. If the tennis player does not have a racket in his hand, he has to throw the ball to other side of the court. What the tennis player has done is that he uses his racket to make a hit as if he is throwing the ball to the other side of the net. He uses an action of hitting to perform a job that is throwing in nature. Of course, he just does what he does as he sees it and as he understands it. He does not have to reason as we are doing here. Because as I mentioned many times before, the actions are part of his human nature; he was born to perform these actions. The important point is that when he hits the ball, does he have the concept of where the ball is going, and how strongly he is thinking that in his mind? Since distance and flying pattern is part of the throwing concept, it will interfere with how the player is going to swing and hit the ball.

Hitting and throwing are similar physically. They are very different mentally. When you hit, you think about here, and you look at contact.

When you throw, you think about there, and you look there. Especially the throwing concept is the most dominating concept in the human mind; it is much stronger than the concept of hitting, even though hitting and throwing are both human survival skills.

Also, the throwing concept is the mother of invention of weapons in human history. The invention of the sling, bows and arrows, guns, rockets, and even the tools of our space exploration today are all coming from the basic throwing concept in our brain.

Now you can see that the tennis game was inherited with a mental trap in itself. No wonder so many intelligent young children are so frustrated when they play tennis. They think that they should be much better than they are, but they are not. When a simple mistake is made, they often yell at themselves, "You're stupid, Grandma can do it." They then smash their rackets. Frustration comes in from not knowing what is wrong and not knowing how to fix it.

Most of the trouble in the game of tennis and golf comes from the players thinking too much and too far ahead of what they do rather than the action itself. This is nature, because we are born that way. This is, however, not healthy when we are playing sports in competition. Therefore, defining the action precisely and concentrating on the action is the only solution.

One action worth a special mention is the concept of throwing. The throwing action associates too closely with the eye function. The eyes are the leaders of any physical action. Mind control is the only solution. In conclusion, concentration is action specific. One action has one concentration. Concentration requires identifying what interferes with your action. Avoiding the interference factors when you execute the actions is the essence of concentration. Defining the athletic actions precisely and pointing out the interference factors is what this book is all about.

This book is written based on the human system. What is the human system? The human system is taking the human as a model system to study, learn, and to emulate how human events should be decided and worked. The human system is the way different parts of the human body work together as a living functional unit physiologically, anatomically, socially, physically, mentally. and psychologically. Humans have the most intelligent system. Humans have the best survival system. It is how great majority of the human population think, work, and live their lives. The human system is humanistic—physiological and philosophical. It is the humanistic way to be a human. It is also precise scientifically. Within the human system, there are numerous subsystems. Every subsystem is operating under the basic principle laid down by the general human system. The general human system is based on the physiological, anatomical, and psychological components of a human body.

Intellectual pursuit and development of sports belong to the natural human trade. Every person is born to be a different athlete. Every person knows how to run, jump, and kick. Every person knows how to catch, hit, and throw. Every person has his/her own athletic potential to be the best he/she can be. Human hand structure gives the anatomical evidence of why humans can catch, hit, and throw. Human foot structure enables humans to run, jump, and kick. Playing tennis, golf, baseball, and soccer are normal human activities. Hands and feet are the most visible hardware that reveal the nature of humans. Without a hand like a human hand and feet like human feet, there will be no sports possible.

Understand that what humans can do is one thing; helping humans to accomplish it the fastest and easiest way possible is another. I am trying to reveal all the mental portions of common sports activities.

Winning is not what you want to win and win. Winning is performing your action properly to win. Actions require concentration. Different actions require different concentration. Concentration is mental.

Mental is what you think. Mental is what you know. Mental is what you feel. Mental is what you see and how you see it. Mental is everything!

1

Why I Am Writing This Book

a. I want people to understand that everybody is born to be an athlete. Everyone has a perfect lower athletic system from one's hips down. Everyone has one's own potential and ability to run, jump, and kick. Everyone has one's own ability to run as fast as one can. Everyone can jump as high as one can. You have a perfect upper athletic system from your hips up. You can push, hit, and throw. Your two athletic systems string together, working seamlessly as a total human athletic system for you to perform all kinds of athletic actions.

b. I want to use the biolink system to remind athletes how to prevent the preventable athletic injuries. Injuries come from overuse and improper use of the human biolink system. Many tennis players get elbow injury. Many baseball players get shoulder injury. Many golf players get back injury. These will all be discussed in the biolink system. Using the biolink system rather than the conventional biomechanics in this book is for that purpose.

c. I want to precisely define the meaning of concentration for athletic actions. Concentration is action specific. Action without concentration is meaningless.

d. I want to help players to develop their skills the fastest way possible. Understanding the mental and physical parameters of an athletic action is required if you want to learn that action as fast as you can. If you want to play tennis or golf as well and as fast as you can, you have to know the mental and physical parameters of the action of hitting and throwing. Most importantly, you have to understand what prevents you from learning as fast as you can and doing the best that you can. You are the only one that can reach your potential. You are also limited by your own potential.

e.   I want to help players to understand the interference factors of the game they are playing. Concentration is to get rid of the interferences. If someone does not know what interferes, how could he/she concentrate?

f.   I want players to be aware that the most detrimental interferences are the intellectual interferences. These types of interferences come from your own intellectual ability. You have to have much deeper mental understanding of the game you play and the actions you perform specifically in order to avoid frustration. Concentration exists on every action. Concentration may be 0 or 100 percent. However, concentration is better for whatever action you perform.

2

Attention, Concentration, and Focus

Different people may feel differently about the meaning of these three words. It is, however, worthwhile to clarify them because each word does play an important role in athletic performance.

Attention, in my mind, is a reminding signal. It is a call for general concentration. It is a call for you to put your mind in a specific area for you to see, to hear, to touch, or to feel. For example, a group of people is getting together; each one is talking with another. Suddenly, you hear "May I have your attention, please?" Then everyone stops talking; it becomes very quiet. Everyone waits to see what is coming up next. In this case, your sense organ, your ear, is ready to hear what is coming up next. Whatever comes up will be something very specific. Whatever comes up is not only an attention process, but it is also a focus process.

In another case, for example, I have ten different objects in one container. The container is covered by a piece of paper. If I want somebody to look into the container and not focus on any one thing particularly, just see the whole thing all together, that means I want him to put his attention on the whole container. This is, in my mind, general attention. When you are in the state of general attention, your eyes are wide open. You are not focusing on any one thing. You can accomplish focusing by slightly moving your eyes.

If you are playing tennis and your opponent is serving, you can see him holding the ball with one hand and moving his racket with another hand. You can also see the court lines on both sides of the net. You are not focused on any one thing particularly but you can see everything.

All three cases above belong to the mental state of attention, or I call them the mental states of general concentration.

Focus is emphasis on the use of the eyes or concentration on one object and one object only. The meaning of focus in sports is more toward the use of the eyes to watch rather than be mindfully inclined. It is very important to learn focus without mental tension. Intense focus with the eyes will delay the time of reaction. When you play tennis, please do not focus on the fast-flying ball. If you focus on a flying ball, you are always going to be later than that flying ball. Focus with mental relaxation is the best way to learn focus.

Concentration implies the ability to isolate the central element from a complex issue. In sports performance, understanding how to perform a specific action is the essence. For any sport action, there are also other factors surrounding this action. The factors could be biomechanical, psychological, neurological, or anatomical. Any one of these factors could contribute to the degree of performance of that specific action. Some of these factors could be interference factors. The process of identifying and isolating these factors is called the process of concentration.

Concentration is action specific. Athletically, concentration is focusing attention toward a single specific action.

Every action has its own concentration. In tennis, concentration on getting to the ball is one concentration. Concentration on making a good tennis stroke is another concentration.

Concentration needs to be learned, practiced, modified if necessary, and mastered.

In order to understand the meaning of concentration precisely, we have to understand the action involved exactly and completely. Identifying the interference factors is the first step to concentration.

The process of concentration is a full mental understanding of the specific athletic action to be performed, and also, understanding all the other factors may interfere with the performance of that action. To isolate the specific athletic action and get rid of those interference factors is the true essence of concentration.

Concentration is not zero and a hundred. However, it is the more, the better. It is necessary to be perfected until it becomes a natural process of that action. Concentration is a specific mental and biomechanical process. It is what you know from your mind and what you do with your body on that specific action and perform that action wholeheartedly and completely without any reservation and without any interference.

3

Physical Survival Actions Become Sports Activities.

When in danger, all animals try to survive. The ability to survive depends on what the animal can do. Survival skills are usually physical activities. These activities are different for different animals. These activities are the nature by birth of that animal system. These activities usually involve both physical and mental components. Physical components are what the animal can do and is doing. The intellectual components are what the animal was thinking at the time when the animal was doing it. We don't know what is on other animals' mind, but we can all see what other animals are doing when they are in danger.

As humans, we also do what we can do to survive. In general, when we are in danger, we run away and we hide. If we cannot run away, we fight. Physically, we fight with our hands and with our feet. Mentally, we think with our head and figure out the best way to survive.

As humans, physically, we have two physical systems, upper and lower. The upper physical system is from the shoulder to the finger. The lower physical system is from the hip to the toe. When we are in danger, we can run away. We can kick with our lower extremities. We can punch, hit with our bare hands. We can also hit with a weapon in our hand. We can also throw an object at our enemy. Now we can understand that the most important and most efficient way to survive is to use a weapon with our *hands*. And the most important weapon to use is to use our head to think. To think is *mental*. This concept tells us how important the *hand* and *mental* ideas are in the *human athletic system*.

The other animals can do with what they have and with what they can when they are in danger. These activities are usually life-and-death struggles.

Human survival skills naturally become exercise and sports activities after social progress and advances in civilization. Since people are born with these capabilities, people feel good when they do it. When physical exercises become competitive sports events, the demand of understanding and level of performance of the physical activity becomes a serious subject matter. Many schools and higher educational institutions offer courses and studies and researches. Many people pursue sports as their lifelong career. Business and merchandise in sports have become very important subjects in our modern society.

4

The Hand Is the Signature
of the Human Race

The human hand is the most important survival organ in the human system. Without the human hand, any human could not even survive for just a few weeks. Back in prehistoric times, fingers were used to grab food to eat. The palm was used to fetch water to drink. Children use their hands to eat once they pass the nursing period. All these are documented historical experiences, and people are still practicing it today.

Human hands and feet are the most powerful body parts to defend and attack. A human uses human hands to protect, and survival is plain and clear. Western-style boxing and Chinese martial arts are typical examples.

From stake swinging and rock throwing to real weapon use, these sports probably have gone through thousands of generations. Later on, knives, spears, and many different weapons were invented and used. All these achievements are due to the fact that humans have human hands.

The human hand can do two things the other primates cannot do. One is holding an elongated object to pock and to swing and to hit. The other is holding a rock to aim and to throw. These two actions are the reasons we can have our sports today.

5

Hand Sports
Are My Favorite

Ping-pong was the only hand game I played when I was a Child. Badminton was not even available for me at the time when I grew up. I am not a very good ping-pong player, but I can play. I know how to hold a ping-pong paddle (with a pen-hold grip). Nobody taught us how to play. As children, we just watch other people play and we play. We feel good when we play, and it becomes quite addictive. This is an indication that sport is part of human nature.

To think about it now, the ping-pong game has greater advantages than a lot of other hand games in terms of physical exercise. It is a real miniature lawn tennis game. It requires fast reaction. It requires a great amount of physical activity. It contains all the physical and mental elements in a real tennis game. If we enlarge the ping-pong table to the size of a tennis court and increase the size and weight of the ping-pong ball to a real tennis ball, we will have to automatically change the size of a ping-pong paddle to a tennis racket and play the game as the tennis game we play today. Even as far the real ping-pong game and tennis game are concerned, there are quite a few mental and biomechanical points in these two games that are very identical. Understand that one game will greatly help to play the other.

6

Why Can Only Humans Play Tennis, Golf, and Baseball?

Hand games were invented hundreds of years ago. Different hand games were played as early as humans have existed. No matter how primitive the games are, they basically contain the mental and physical characteristics of the hand games. Games are basically evolutionary in nature. Humans can only do what humans can do, and humans can only use what humans can provide. Early games and present games are quite different. They all follow the progress of time. Even the invention, progress, and modification of the game of ping-pong need volumes of books to describe its history. The modern games of tennis, golf, and baseball today are all the results from the evolution of early inventions of these games historically.

Humans have coexisted with all other primates like monkeys, gorillas, and chimpanzees for millions of years. Why have we never observed any other primates play hand games like humans do? The answer is, "The other primates do not have a brain like the human brain, and the other primates do not have a hand like the human hand." I learned all these after I discovered the hand structure and its relation to sport activities.

7

How Did I Get into
the Subject of Hands?

The subject of the human hand has been studied extensively through the years. My involvement with this subject is pure accidental. It is the result of my discovery of the hand structure that, as I proposed, is the only anatomical evidence of why humans are born to be natural throwers and also natural hitters with an extended implement in their hands. Of course, we all know humans can throw and hit, but we do not know why. Now we have the answer.

Being born to be throwers and hitters indicates how strongly the concepts of throwing and hitting are buried deep in the human mind. These hitting and throwing become human nature. If hitting interferes with your throwing or throwing interferes with your hitting, it can be a very serious problem for athletic performance. This is exactly the case today in sports such as tennis, golf, baseball, and/or other sport events. This is the reason why I use the intellectual interference to represent this kind of interference. Now let me explain how I got into this subject.

The hand is part of my body. I know what I can do with my hand. However, I never gave too much thought about my hand except at times when I hurt my hand.

I have two children, two boys. They were born in the middle sixties. I like sports. You make friends during sports activities, so I like them to participate in sports also. We encourage them to do all kinds of physical activities. They tried swimming, baseball, basketball, football, and all other physical programs the Ann Arbor local community could offer. They got into tennis also.

Compared with other sports, tennis is a noncontact sport. It is safer from a parent's point of view. We feel more comfortable when they are on a tennis court.

To my surprise, tennis is a different animal compared to other sports. It is an individual sport. Individual competition depends solely on individual performance. The lives of participants are suddenly changed. The ideas of winning, losing, physical abilities, intellectual qualities, and self-esteem all become big deals in the player's mind. Parents are pushed into it voluntarily or involuntarily.

Well-to-do families hire private coaches and go to private clubs; daily private lessons become routine activities. As a concerned parent and a struggling PhD candidate in school at that time, I too could not overlook my children's activities. However, I was not able to help my children physically, intellectually and financially because tennis is not my cup of tea. My children did take a few group lessons with other kids, and I was always there to watch. So I had a general idea of what the game is and how the coaches are teaching and what the kids are learning. Nevertheless, my intention to help my children never wavered, even though I did not know how at that moment and I could not afford to hire private coaches either. But tennis occupied my mind most of the time.

This is one comment I often heard from tennis coaches at that time: if you make a mistake in your game, *check your grip*. I understand that the hand and the handle of the tennis racket are directly connected for sure, but I did not have any idea of the types of tennis grips players use in competition. I did believe, though, that hands and grips must be very important to the game. To understand the hand and tennis grips became my priority. I have even tried to invent a better racket for my own children to use. From then on, the words "hand and grip" were stocked into my mind. I, however, knew nothing about the *hand* theoretically. I started to feel that it is something I have to learn. It is not just only related to the game of tennis; it is a very important part of the *human system.*

Search to Find the Answer in Proper Tennis Grips

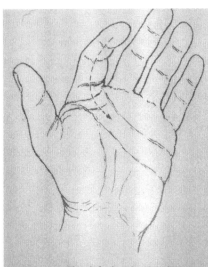

FIG. 4. The left hand, showing the functional creases which appear on flexion of the index finger, the direction of which corresponds to the interspace between the distal crease of the hand and the thenar crease. The long axis of the index finger in flexion corresponds to this interspace. The flexion creases of the index finger run across this space. The broken line indicates the direction of the finger singly flexed.

The first thing I did then was to go to the university medical library to look for the subject, *hand.*

I was totally overwhelmed with the amount of material covering the subject of the hand. After a few weeks reviewing the anatomy of the hand structure, I knew I was working in the wrong direction. Even though I had gotten a superficial knowledge of the hand structure, there was nothing I could see related to the use of the hand, especially related to how to hold a tennis racket.

I then switched into the subject of *human hand function.* The first book I checked out was *Kaplan's Functional and Surgical Anatomy of the Hand* by Kaplan, published by the J. B. Lippincott Company in 1965. I thought with the name *Functional and Surgical Anatomy of the Hand* I should be able to get some functional information about the hand. That book is a classical surgical text for medical professionals and written by a highly respected hand expert. To my surprise, it was unexpected, and I found a mistake in that book. As shown in figure 1, at the left, Dr. Kaplan explained that the flexion of the index finger is flexed in the direction of the interspace of the distal flexion crease and the proximal flexion crease. However, if you try to do it, you will find that it is absolutely impossible for the index finger to flex in that direction and between that space. When the index finger is fully flexed, it will naturally flex onto the thinner eminence.

Finding something not true in the medical library was a big surprise to me because majority of my life was spent in the library and I put my life of trust in everything I read there. I have never questioned anything I read in any library before. Beside this picture, Dr. Kaplan also proposed a hand structure. He divides the hand into three parts, as shown in the picture, figure 3. I started to feel that hand structure may also need some further investigation. This thought led me into a long detour of my life. It's all because of my own curiosity; I want to find out what is the right answer.

9

Dr. Kaplan Confirmed My Finding

The above picture is from Dr. Kaplan's book on page 6. We call this picture figure 1. Here, you can see the written explanation under the picture from Dr. Kaplan's book. At that moment, I simply feel that the flexion crease may not a have close relationship with the physiological structure of the human hand, and I would never doubt that Dr. Kaplan's understanding about the human hand function has missed something. I also feel that there must be a gap between understanding the human hand structure and human hand function. Hand surgeons know everything about the physiological structure of the hand. They probably never tried to figure out how the hand function theoretically should be, because nobody knows how to use their hand better than a good hand surgeon. That is the reason I think the misinterpretation of the hand function of the flexure lines in Dr. Kaplan's book happened.

Since intellectual information has to be interpreted properly, I thought somebody had to do something to correct this information. To find out something wrong is easy, and to correct some misinterpretation requires in-depth understanding of that subject. Jumping into a subject I knew nothing about was a big mistake.

That was in the late seventies. Through great effort, I did get a chance to contact Dr. Kaplan and asked him about the picture in his book. He did it with me on the phone and he said, "I could not do it either." He also mentioned that as hand surgeons, their main concern and study was on the physiological structures such as bones, muscles, and nerves. He felt bad about this mistake, and he thanked me for my call. I thanked him for talking to me.

After the brief conversation with Dr. Kaplan, I felt that I had to do something about this matter. This turned my life practically upside down for many years. My primary goal of helping my children in tennis also included learning how the human hand works and also why the index finger was not doing what Dr. Kaplan indicated.

10

I Got into a Field I Was Not Prepared for

The struggle to find the correct answer is a long and painstaking one. There were no books on the human hand functions I could read to give me any helpful information. There was no hand surgeon whom I knew could give me any reasonable answer. During that period, I did ask a few surgeons about these questions; there was nobody who could come up with any proper explanation. They all said, "It is good you found the mistakes. I agree with you that Dr. Kaplan was wrong on this subject." Nobody seemed interested in this too much. I have a sense that everybody thought, *That is a minor mistake, so what?* My feeling at that time was I was not comfortable to know any misinformation of a major subject was staying in the medical library and people were doing nothing about it. I thought that way at that time. You can tell how naive I was when I was young.

Actually, I did not need them to confirm the little fact that there was a mistake in the book. I wanted them to give me some proper explanation about hand function I could help my kids to play tennis. Obviously, it is unavoidable that a certain amount of misinformation probably exists concerning many subjects in many different fields in the libraries today.

In 1984, many Dr. Kaplan's former students had a conference to honor and remember Dr. Kaplan's accomplishments and contribution in the field of hand surgery. Dr. Morton Spinner edited a new edition of Dr. Kaplan's book. Unfortunately, the same pictures and the misinterpretation of the information are still there today. This is the story when and how I got into the subject of the hand.

To think about it now, curiosity is not a bad thing. What I searched then was the best way to hold the tennis racket. I found it was not only that. I also found a proper hand structure, the origin of sports in general, the essence of the mental aspect of the sports actions, and how important the human hand was in relation to human nature.

11

A Long, Difficult Journey Finally Ended

Finding a problem and not solving it is not my nature. So I was trapped in a long, difficult struggle. It lasted more than five years. I looked at my hand day and night. My own hand is the only object I could use at any time, at any place. I watched my hand movement for thousands of hours. I really did not know what to look for. The misinterpretation of Dr. Kaplan's book was very obvious and clear. What else could I do? There was no clear vision on this subject for me to look forward to and work on. I just felt that something was not right.

After a longtime observation of my own hand, palm creases were the only things that caught my attention because palm creases were the only things I faced. In China, palm creases were used by fortune-tellers to tell people's fortune. I started to feel there must be some close connection between the hand structure and function and the nature of humans themselves. Human hands, like language, are part of the expression apparatus to expose humans in action. So I started to concentrate on the nature of the palm creases in human life. I realized that palm creases simply represent the bony movement underneath the skin. The palm creases helped me figure out how human hands worked. Thousands of hours searching for the importance of human hand function came from watching my own hand.

Through more than five years of searching, I finally found all the answers. I have found the proper gross hand structure. In figure 2, I have proposed a hand structure and compared it with the hand structure proposed by Dr. Kaplan. Even though there is only a minor difference in its appearance, there are tremendous differences in their function and complication. It makes me understand that it is not just the hand structure; it reveals what humans really are like. Now, from the proper human hand structure and functions, I have a clear understanding of how important the role the human hand plays in the development of human society and human civilization. From understanding the past, we can have a proper perspective of the future. We can understand where sports come from and why only humans can do the things human do. Of course, the human hand is only the hardware; without the proper soft ware, the hardware does not mean anything. However, without the proper hardware, the software does not do anything either. Now, we understand why all the primates are different—because they have different hand structure and can do different things with their hands. To understand that the athletic actions are part of human nature is very important, because this has tremendous implication with sports psychologists.

Just the picture of human hand structure and the independent extension of the single index finger tell me all the stories about what humans can do and why humans are the kings on the plain earth. From the hand structure, we learn what humans can do.

There are a few important results from my search related to human hand structure and functions I am going to list here:

1. A proper human hand structure was finally reached.
2. The origins of the sports tennis, golf, baseball, etc., came from human hand structure.
3. The actions of hitting, throwing, and catching are all basic athletic actions humans were born to do.
4. The human hand is the most important hardware of the human system.
5. Humans have a complete circular eye-hand repetitively creative learning system.
6. The human hand is armed with a powerful precision and power system.
7. The human hand clearly reveals human nature and the future of humans.

12

A Hand Structure Was Proposed
The extension of the hand plays a role
in the survival of the human race.
The flexion of the hand is responsible
for advancement of civilization.

a.   An open hand has significant meaning.

Dr. Kaplan's interpretation of the index finger was a very simple mistake. He simply considered how the index finger was flexed and never thought of what happens while the index finger is extended and what the extension of the index fingers means in the human system. This is very natural because, in general, people always think that the most important function of the hand is to form a grip to grasp things. We seldom pay attention to people when they open their hands except when we are ready to shake other people's hands. The real meaning of an extended arm and an open hand in human life has never been seriously considered philosophically or functionally. Sometimes, people slap their children with an open hand when they tell lies. Sometimes people pat on their friend's back with an open hand. We do open our hand if we hold something for too long and we need to rest our fingers. There is really not much to see with an open hand. When you open your hand, all you can see are the extended fingers. What else can we see if we are not reading palms? It is hard to imagine what else is worth looking for and studying. However, the human hand is much more than we generally thought superficially. The open hand and closed hand have a tremendous neurological relationship in interpreting human emotions when we talk or make speeches. The human hand is the most important hardware connecting between our brain and our eyes. The human hand is the real performer of whatever we can do for survival in the human system. We can do pretty much of anything we think unless something is too far to reach, too heavy to lift, too soft to hold, too hot to touch, or too big to grab. Actually, the human hand can create things to overcome many things we cannot accomplish directly with our bare hand.

In my mind, closing the hand to form grips and the open arm and the open hand with extended fingers are two equally important subjects that need to be studied and investigated. The most important concept of the extended arm and the open hand is to understand that the open hand is the basis of the human system to face the outside world. If we cannot open, we cannot hold. If we cannot open our hand, we cannot release to throw. The shoulder joint and the elbow joint are just responsible to push and carry the hand to the proper location in time to perform any job assigned by the brain. The wrist is the primary joint to operate the hand. Without the pronation and supination and flexion and extension of the wrist, humans can do very little of anything, including sports. Without the flexion and extension of the flanges of the fingers, human can never play music and write or even use utensils.

When people speak, there is always hand gestures used to express people's minds. We can understand how closely the mind is connected to our hand. In our hand gestures, the hand motions usually represent the actions are taken. Therefore, to understand the human hand, just the grasp forming is not enough. Of course it is not the job of any hand surgeon to understand every aspect of the human hand. I think this is the reason why Dr. Kaplan never considered the extension of the index finger or the significance of the open hand. As a matter of fact, the mental implication of the open hand has never been studied. From the hand gesture in speeches and lecturing, we can understand the importance of the open-handed sign in mutual communication.

We have talked about the mental part of the open hand and the extension of the fingers. Now let's consider some aspects of the functions of the hand grips. There are basically two important kinds of human hand grips that need to be understood. One is the power grip; the other is the precision grip.

b. Power Grip

When you form a fist with an empty hand or hold an implement with force, you are using a power grip. This can be shown in figure 2.

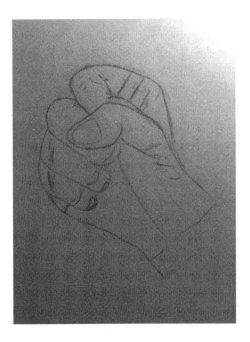

When we form a fist with an open hand, it is a power grip. When you hold a baseball bat to hit a baseball, that is a power grip. When you hold a tennis racket to play tennis, that is a power grip. Just from the name, we can understand that the power grip involves a whole hand to form a grip in action. The power grip is for our hand to engage in a heavier implement to do a heavier job. In all the cases, the direction of extension of the implement in the power grip is in line with the extension of the index finger when all the fingers are fully extended. A slight ulnar deviation of the wrist will line up the direction of the implement with the direction of the forearm. It is the most favorable direction for using the implement in the action of hitting in any upper athletic performance. The power grip involves using of force, using force related to survival. All the human physical survival skills are based on the use of the power grip with various implements. This is the very basis of our upper-extremity sports today.

c.   Precision Grip

The precision grip can be shown in figure 4.

When we use utensils such as forks, spoons, or chopsticks to eat, we use a precision grip. When we use tools, we use a precision grip. When we use pipettes in a chemistry laboratory, we use a precision grip. When we use small tool, we use a precision grip. The thumb, index finger, and the middle finger forming a tripod structure is the most delicate and precise structure for holding and operating in our daily life. The precision grip is the reason humans can develop into a civilized society. The invention of tools and the development of science are all the results of the ability of the human hand to use the precision grip.

When you open your hand, you see a few palm creases. When you close your hand, you can see the hand slowly folding along those creases. It is easier to see a grip is forming and the hand can hold something. You can see the hand is at work, and you can see all the fingers are at work. All the functional creases are at work right in front of your eyes. By fully examining the functional creases, one can know and see how the hand is working. The distal transverse palm crease, D, indicates that the middle, ring, and little fingers work together as a unit favorably when forming a full-handed power grip. At the same time, when you close your hand to form a full-hand power grip, your index finger will automatically come together with the other three fingers. It can also stay in the extended direction and not come together with the other fingers. That means the index finger has its own freedom and choice. It can help enhance the power grip, or it can control and guide the direction of extension of the object the hand is holding. If we want to extend our arm to a certain direction or point at something in a certain direction, we want to use our index finger for precision and control. That is why we often call the index finger the pointer. It depends on what the person wants to do with the object in the hand.

The thumb will fold following the radial longitudinal palm crease (R). The main opposing action of the thumb is the middle finger. The ring and little fingers are the helpers of the middle finger. That is the reason we always snap our fingers using the thumb and the middle finger.

The overlap of the proximal transverse palm crease (P) and the radial longitudinal palm crease (R) shows the importance of the thumb. The thumb has a dual function. It can come together with the index finger to form a very delicate pinch grip, like you want to pick up a needle from a flat surface. The thumb can also form the power grip with the middle, ring, and little fingers, such as when you close your hand and use your index finger to point at something.

If you check on the hand structure I provide, you can understand that when all the fingers are fully extended, you can see that the index finger is extended in the interspace between the proximal transverse palm crease (P) and the radial longitudinal palm crease (R). This is true, just as Dr. Kaplan has indicated. The area covered by the black shaded lines as shown in my drawing is called the hand proper. All the fingers can fold over and pass this area but not necessarily into this area. This area is reserved for some object we want to hold or go grab in our hand.

The area covered by the red color, including the thumb, the muscle, and the bones under the skin, is the thenar eminence. The area covered by the green color is called ulnae, which includes the middle, ring, and little finger and the muscles and bones. The main function of the hand is the opposing action between the green and the red area. Here I want to give you an example. If we look at the hand as a shoe, the fingers are like the shoelace. Only difference is that the hand requires one string on one side and needs four strings on the other side. For very small object, we can use one string on one side and use one string on the other side. We can hold objects of different shapes and different sizes. We can hold a small object as small as a pea; we can hold an object as big as a large apple. We can hold an object as thin as a needle; we can hold an object as thick as a baseball bat. The thumb can form a pinch grip with the index finger, such as when you pick up a needle from the surface of a table. The thumb can also form different grips with any other finger on the other side of the hand.

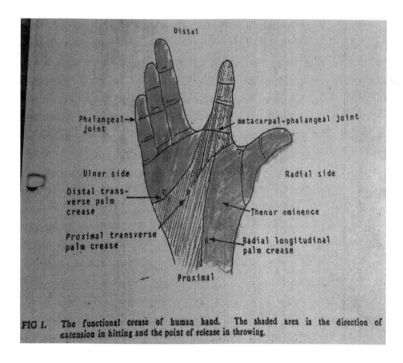

FIG I.   The functional crease of human hand.   The shaded area is the direction of extension in hitting and the point of release in throwing.

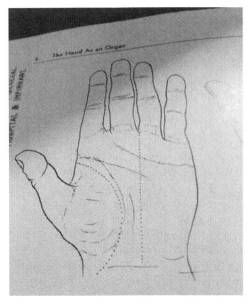

Figure 3. Comparison of Dr. Kaplan's hand
structure at the bottom and my proposed
hand structure.

As shown in the above picture, the closing of the red (the thumb) and
the green area, the power grip is formed. A tennis racket or a golf club
can be held in there. The precision grip is the closing of the thumb, the
index, and the middle fingers. You can hold a pen to write this way.
In the field of hand surgery, everybody knows that the thumb is the
most important finger in the human hand. It is very obvious because
on one side of the hand, we have four fingers that can work, and on the
opposing side, there is only one finger. Without the opposing thumb, we
cannot form a grip. We also know that the thumb can form a grip with
any one of the fingers on the other side. This is the reason everybody
knows that the opposing thumb is the most important finger of the
hand.

The difference of the extension and flexion of all the fingers to form
all kinds of grips is obvious, but the direction of extension of the index
finger and the open space represented by the range of motion of the index
finger reveals tremendous information of the human hand structure and
the human hand function. Without this open space represented by the

extended index finger, the human race would be just like other primates in the jungle. There will be no human civilization. It would be a world of no sports. It is important for us to know why and how the flexion and extension of a human hand contribute to the human civilization and culture. The reason I am stressing on the extension of the index finger is that the index finger is the main difference between human hands and the hands of other primates. This is the reason I call the index finger one of the principal human-specific characteristic signs. No other primates can extend their index finger independently like a human does.

13

The Extension of the Index Finger Shows the Direction of Extension of an Implement in Hitting, and It Is also the Direction of Releasing in Throwing

We have just discussed that our hands can hold a very small object like a small glass bead. Our hands can also hold a large ball. What happens when we hold a long stick or a long object like a tennis racket? We know that this long object has to extend out of our hand. When we hold part of the long object in our hand, there will be an extra-long portion extending out of our hand. We call the part in our hand as the handle. We usually hold the handle with a power grip. We have to use the thumb on one side and four fingers on the other side to maintain firmness and balance. Since the tennis racket is too long, it must be extended outside the hand, then this long object will extend through the opening between the thumb and the index finger of the hand. When we want to form a power grip with our hand to hold the handle of something, the index finger will automatically come together with the middle finger, the ring finger, and the little finger as a group on one side of the hand to form a power grip with the thumb on the other side of the hand. The index finger can also touch the racket handle independently and make sure the racket is pointed at the right target. The direction of extension of the index finger in the hand structure represents the sense of direction of the object extending from our hand. This is the special feature of the human hand. This is how humans are made. With this feature, it allows the human hand to hold on an object and to make a swing motion to hit. With our hand structure, it allows the hand to hold objects of different sizes and lengths. This long object has to be laid in the black shaded area, as shown in my hand structure. This black area is what I called the hand proper. The hand proper is synchronized with the wrist. Any object in the hand proper will be in line with the direction of the forearm when making an offensive action in fighting. This the most favorable position for the object to be held in the hand. The length of the object can be held depending on the strength of the person who can maintain the stability and balance to operate this object. Children use short, light tennis rackets, and adults use long and heavy tennis rackets. With the guidance of the index finger, we can swing this long object aimed at another object at a certain distance away. This is basically the hitting action, and the grip is called the power grip.

In a similar fashion, with a slightly modified power grip, we can hold a ball, a stone, a piece of metal in our hand. Then the whole body can make a specific physical movement to accelerate the upper extremity and let the object in the hand be released from the hand in a specific trajectory and in the direction of the extended index finger and aim at any specific object a certain distance away. This is a powerful throwing action. It is like a pitcher pitching a baseball. The range of the throwing action depends on the thrower's ability to accelerate his upper extremity before the releasing motion. The type of trajectory and the range of throw are programmed in the human brain. This throwing action is also with a power grip. This is the distance related to the defensive and offensive mechanisms of humans. We can understand how powerful it is in the animal kingdom.

14

Tennis Grips

After working so long to find out what the proper tennis grips are, I realized that the proper tennis grip was really blown out of its portion. Of course, I am saying this now because I understand the hand structure and the game and everything about this problem. However, what I am saying is quite true. I remember many years ago, Mr. Arthur Ashe in New York did raise the grip question to me. I used a wood tennis racket with a modified grip to show him that we play tennis is with our hands and we seldom think about the racket. However, to have a racket with the proper size of grip to fit the player's hand is the most important part of the game. We use the geometrical shape of the racket handle to synchronize with our hand, and changing grip in different shots is just as easy as a simple switch of our fingers. For example, if you want to change a forehand grip to a continental grip, it is just like blinking your eyes. You know, you can use a continental grip to do almost everything in a tennis game.

Now we can talk about the proper ways to hold a tennis racket. It was really a long, long detour for me to learn about how to hold a tennis racket. Anyway, I did gain deeper understanding of how a human hand conforms to human behavior and how the human hand relates to human nature.

It is true that every coach who teaches tennis always teaches the students how to hold a tennis racket to begin with. The types of grips are many.

There is the eastern forehand grip, eastern backhand grip, semiwestern forehand grip, western forehand grip, continental grip, and two-handed backhand grip. People used to use different hand positions on the handle to call different grips. It was very complicated and confusing.

I think the best way to teach the grip is to teach how the hand works. Basically, everybody knows how to use his or her hand to hold something. The first person who played the game never worried about knowing how to hold his racket. He just used the racket to hit an incoming ball according to what he thought and what he wanted. Holding the racket one way is not necessarily the best way to hit the ball because the ball may come from different directions and different height. By changing the way of holding the racket, one can hit the ball efficiently and comfortably until one knows what is the best way to hold the racket under different situations. This learning process requires some time. Therefore, to teach the grips to new learners is necessary. It will save some time. This is why coaches have taught different grips in tennis.

However, the way of teaching tennis grips should be different. It is better to teach tennis grips according to how the human hand works. When holding something in our hand, we are integrating the object we are holding in our hand into one system. We know where it is extended to, and we know which direction it is facing. The tennis racket handle is such a good design with clearly identifiable surfaces to represent different directions.

Now our hands work in such a way in the neurological system—the motor neurons are in the palm, and the sensory neurons are on the fingers. It is for the palm to hold and for the fingers to feel. On the racket handle, there are flat surfaces. Some surfaces are synchronized with the racket surface, and some surfaces have an angle with the racket surface. To know the surface of the racket, we can understand which direction and at what angle we can contact the ball. This is absolutely required when we play tennis. According to our hand structure and function, we can classify the tennis grips into the following:

  a. Forehand grip. When you hold your racket handle, the first thing you should notice that there are different surfaces on the handle. Usually, you even do not have to look; once you hold the racket, you will feel with your hand. When I say you feel it. It is very important, because from then on, everything you do is how you feel it. There are two flat surfaces; one is synchronized with the string of the racket on one side, and the other is synchronized with the string surface on the other side. It simply means if the ball comes from one side, you hit the ball with one side of the racket, and if the ball comes from the other side, you use the other side of the string to contact the ball. If the ball comes from your left side and you are a right-handed person, you use your racket to hit the ball to your left. The way you hold your racket is called the forehand grip. If you want to hit the ball with your total body effort biomechanically, your forehand grip should be like this: let your little finger, ring finger, and middle finger together feel the flat surface of the racket handle, which is synchronized with the surface of the racket face directly to the incoming ball. Don't pay too much attention to your thumb. The thumb also plays a minor role in controlling the racket. Your forefinger is primarily to feel the direction of the extension of the racket and to help you to control the racket to make a shot.

b. Two-handed backhand grip. If you are a right-handed person and the ball comes from your right side, you put your left hand in front of your right hand and hold the racket handle as if you were a left-handed person using a forehand grip with your left hand. This is a two-handed backhanded grip. The two-handed backhand grip is essentially a left-handed forehand grip with the right hand as a helper to cooperate with and balance your hitting action. In a two-hand back grip, the right hand only plays a minor role. There are three different ways the right hand can hold the racket handle; it can be a forehand, backhand, or continental grip. None of these are critically important. In general, however, the right hand uses a continental grip. We can reasonably say that a two-handed backhand grip is essentially a left-handed forehand grip. The middle finger, the ring finger, and the little finger of the left hand feel the flat surface of the front of the racket handle. That gives information about the hitting surface of the racket. The wrist, elbow, shoulder, and hip will do all the rest of the work to execute the shots.

c. One-handed backhand grip. If you are a righthanded person and you see a ball coming in from your right and you plan to hit a one-handed backhand, put your palm on top of the racket handle and put your thumb and the thenar eminence against the flat surface of the back of the racket handle. The main idea is to feel the flat surface with your thumb on the backside of your racket handle. Use your index finger to feel the flat surface on the opposite side of the racket handle. It uses the red-colored portion of the hand structure to push the racket up in a top-spin backhand stroke.

d. Continental grip. The continental grip is a grip between the forehand grip and the backhand grip. It is an all-around grip. It uses your thumb to feel one flat side of the racket handle and your index finger to feel the opposite side the racket handle. It is absolutely necessary to use this grip for the one-handed underspin shot because your hand has the maximum control of the racket, and also, your arm is at the most comfortable position to make contact with the ball. It is also absolutely necessary to use this grip to serve.

e. Western and semiwestern grip. The pure western grip is not a very favorable one in my mind. Many young players develop into a western grip because when they play tennis at very young age, the racket's handle is too big for their small hands. When a small hand holds a big racket grip, in the player's mind, he is using a forehand grip, but in reality, he/she is using a western grip. When the hands get bigger, it modifies automatically into a semiwestern grip. What I am trying to say is that the grips are related to the hand size and the size of the handle. Usually, holding a smaller handle is better. You can use one grip to do almost everything in the game. So as far as the grip is concerned, feeling the racket handle with the fingers is the real accurate way to decide the type of grips one is to use. Actually, knowing how the hand works is the best way to understand what different grips mean.

15

Human and Computer

At this stage of my life, I think I do know humans better than I know computers. I went through more than eighty years' human life experience, but I never had a single year of formal computer education. No matter how hard humans try, I do not think humans can ever build a robot more intelligent than humans. Computer may have multiple capabilities over some human limitations, but where overall intellectual potential is concerned, humans are the upper limit. Even though a computer can never reach the level of human intelligence, I still want to use the computer as a model for people to understand humans.

Yes, the human body is a computer—not an ordinary computer but an almighty biological computer. No people can ever make this computer except a man and a woman or by using a human egg to make this computer in a different way.

In this biological computer, the brain stores all the software. The brain is protected within the thick head bone. The whole body, inside and out, is the complete integrated hardware. The most important part of the hardware of this biological computer is the *hand*. The software is stored in the brain, and it is absolutely numberless. It is absolutely impossible to number the software programs because any program can be created, changed, modified, and improved at an instant blink of the eyes, diffusion of the eyes, or slight movement of the eyes. The eyes serve as a program changer. There are five different channels (five senses) to collect new information for programming. Any program, even in progress, can be changed, modified, or canceled and new programs created. This is a continuous dynamic process. This is how humans work. Do computers work this way too?

We emphasize our brain so much that we, indeed, overlook the importance of our hands. Human hands have such a simple structure, but with its ability to protect the human body and its ability to teach the brain to program and reprogram everything in human life, the hand does plays the dominant protective role in the integrated human system. Without the hand and upper-extremity link system, humans would be like a group of little dolphins living on the land.

Practically speaking, the human body does work like a computer. Just the hand really can do nothing; however, when it hooks up with the brain, the system can do anything. The hand is not just doing something, but it is also directly communicating with the brain. It seems the brain and the hand have emerged together as one neurological system. If we want to do something with our hand, then there must be a part of the brain that provides that information for our hand to do. At the same time, if we are doing something with our hand, there must be a part of our brain that thinks about what we are doing. Our brain provides the initial working order. The hand carries out that order. The brain constantly thinks about and evaluates the ongoing process. The hand will continuously modify and improve the ongoing process until the work is well done. Here, actually, we can say that the brain and hand are just one thing and linked together through our neuromuscular system. Of course, we can never overlook the role our eyes play in the whole process. Without the eyes, it is only a slow touching process. The eyes are the leader dogs of the blind. The hand is a doer, but it is blind. In tennis, we have to know clearly that the eye is the leader of any action. Only the brain can control eye function. Without mind training, the eye always leads the action.

16

Biological Progression

The living biological system progresses according to its own naturally given ability. That means living things live with what they have; living things learn and improve with what they can. Human race and human society is the most obvious such system. Just by imagining how the world was one hundred years ago and how the world is now, we will understand what biological progression means to humans. For all other systems, I assume they will be following the same principles; however, I am not knowledgeable enough to discuss the situation. I do believe the principle of biological progression should hold true for all the living systems because all life forms want to be alive.

A human has the most intelligent life form. It also has the most sophisticated and complicated living system. The most important thing in humans is that humans can learn, adapt, change, create, receive, and give. All these abilities are due to the unlimited number of software programs in the human brain as we mentioned in the last chapter, and also, human have powerful upper and lower athletic systems as their hardware. Humans can use the five neurological senses to collect information and think and improve whatever humans can do. The human is the only animal with everything changed and improved with time. Just think how human conditions are ten thousand, five thousand, two thousand, one thousand, five hundred, one hundred, even fifty years ago and what the human conditions are now on every level of the human society.

Biological progression plays a major role in what the human race is and what human society has become today. Biological progression is essentially evolutionary. In order to improve and progress, we must have the ability to start something to begin with. All the sports programs today are primarily developed from the primitive human survival skills in the past. Those capabilities of the human race struggling to live have developed into activities people enjoy today.

As we mentioned before, sports activities are basically fighting skills. Fighting skills are survival skills. Even the concept of survival has been modified through the principle of *biological progression* somewhat. We used to just think survival was self-survival. Now, we gradually understand that *survival should be mutual survival*, not only self-survival. We, as humans, should clearly understand that to stop killing each other and help each other to survive is the only way to preserve the human race. At the same time, protecting other systems from being extinguished from the earth is the responsibility only humans can perform.

Humans are born to throw. The throw concept is imprinted in the human brain. The biomechanics are very complicated. It takes a few years for a child to develop. The human arm is structured to perform the throwing action. When people could not throw as far as one wanted, then the bow and arrow were invented. The basic concept of throwing is to release something and to make it fly from here to there.

Gunpowder was invented in China thousands of years ago. Gunpowder, fireworks, guns, and rockets are all based on the principle of biological progression. Even the space of exploration today is all based on the fact that humans are born with the concept of throwing. The throwing skill is so important that it is still the most dominating action in sports today. We can understand the role a baseball pitcher plays in baseball or the role of a quarterback plays in the game of American football. Without the concept of throwing and the arm structure of a human, there will be no sports in humans at all.

Humans know how to hit with a stick, so the spears, swords, and many long and extended forms of weapons were invented.

Humans knows how to catch, so many different traps were invented. However, catch is basically running, and bicycles were invented.

Now, I want to take the mystery of the word *brain* out of our minds somewhat. We know that the brain is just a large piece of tissue in our body system with different structures and functions. It is protected in the head bone and everybody just calls it *brain*. Assume we have never seen a picture of brain tissue before. It is just hidden in the skull, and nobody knows how it looks. Now, if we wanted to draw a picture to show what the brain looks like neurologically and visually, the picture will be exactly like the human body inside and out. It is just like what a human looks like. Every part of our body is represented by a piece of brain tissue. Now we know, when we see a picture of a human hand, there will be a piece of brain tissue that contains all the information of what the hand is and what the hand can do. However, we can see the hand, touch the hand, shake the hand, and watch the hand at work. Actually, when we say we can watch how the hand works, our brain already knows clearly how the job is progressing and what the next step should be. So as far as the brain and hand are concerned, they form a progressive learning-thinking-working progressive cycle. This cycle can be stalled, stopped, or restarted. This is what I call biological progression. This is seemingly the only special ability of humans in the primate world. Even though I am trying to use the computer to illustrate how the human system works, in reality, all the computers and artificial intelligence are attempts to build machines as smart as humans. However, we all know that a human can never build a machine exactly like a human.

17

Eye-Hand Coordination and Eye-Hand Cooperation

It is apparent that all the progress in humans is the result of the inseparable partnership of the human eyes and the human hands. This is the full eye-hand cooperation learning process cycle.

In the upper-extremity sports activities, the final direct performing member is always the hand. In the action of catching, the hand has to make the contact. In the action of hitting, the hand has to make the contact (or the hand holding an implement has to make the contact). In the action of throwing, the hand has to make the final release. No matter how much our body works to perform that action, the action will not be complete until the hand finishes what the hand is supposed to do.

Let's turn to the extension of the index finger. This is the difference between the human hand and the hands of all other primates. When our hand is fully extended, the direction of extension of the index finger is the sense of direction in the human system. The index finger is usually called the pointer. It represents the natural direction of extension of the forearm in an overhanded throwing action. The index finger is synchronized with the eye function if we want to use our hand to indicate the direction we are thinking about. This is part of the eye-hand coordination in terms of direction determination. Of course, we can try to avoid using the index finger deliberately and use other fingers to point in any direction. But this is not what our body is designed for. If Dr. Kaplan had said that the index finger is extended in the space rather than flexed in the space as he mentioned, everything would be perfectly fine. The index finger is usually the finger we use when we want to point to a specific direction or a specific object. That is the reason we usually call the index finger the Pointer. With the index finger as a human has, a human is able to make the action of throwing in the human system. Without the index finger as a human has, a human could never play tennis, baseball, golf, and all other upper-extremity sports.

The conventional way to study the human hand functions is always to study how the fingers form what kinds of grips. Of course, grips are important. It is just like this: I have so many strings—what kinds of nuts can I tie? This is exactly what all other primate grips are for. Their grips are simply to grab things for their needs. For humans, the grips are not just for us to grip things to eat like using utensils. We can grip things to feed other people or animals. The tendency and inclination of an open hand or extended finger are the basic human intellectual capacity to deal with the outside world. We use pens to write. We hold tools to work. Even the actions of hitting and throwing also involve the forming of grips. If you cannot grab, you cannot hit with an implement. If you cannot hold, you will not have anything to throw. However, the implications of "open the hand" or "extend your finger" have much more.

The hand does all the work. The eye watches how the hand is doing. They are not just in coordination; they are working as a team. It is close cooperation. Just like a leader dog and a blind person, they are a team at work. This is the way the human body works. Usually, the eye always leads to where the action is going. This is the reason whenever a tennis player hits a ball, you tend to look where the ball is going. If you ever have the concept of throwing or placement concept in your mind, when you hit a ball, you have a hard time keeping your eye completely on the contact when you hit. Once your eye moves, your mind changes, then your swing is compromised.

18

Animal Survival Skills
Are Sports Actions

a.   The Action of Catching

We do not know what the environment of the prehistoric times is like. We are assuming that it is similar to the African jungle today. One thing we know for sure is that there was no modern civilization. Everything was as primitive as it could be.

In the world, then, many kinds of animals were present. Like life today, survival is the key. Humans, of course, were also somewhere there. All the jungles are similar to present jungles, and there are jungles and jungles everywhere. Strong and fast animals eat the weaker and slower animals. The strongest and fastest animals become the kings. Ecologically, it follows the basic survival rules in the animal kingdom. The human must be also present but only living in some inhabitable places. Humans survive the human way. Some animals cohabit with humans like what we have today. Wild animals primarily use the ability to run to catch and to run to escape from their prey. What I am trying to say is that running is the most physical part of the animal activities. If it is true for other animals, it is also true for humans. If we look at all the sports activities today, there is not a single good athlete who is a better than the average runner except in some nonrunning sports like golf. In tennis, running is the most physical part of the game. We call that the first action in tennis games.

As humans, we catch with our hands. We have our eye-hand coordination. Animals catch with their mouths. They have their eye-mouth coordination. For flying objects, humans can catch more easily than other animals because humans know how to make traps; for running objects, the other animals can catch better than us.

The physical part of the catching action is running. There is also a mental ingredient in the execution of that action. How to start running requires thought and the function of the eyes. These are the mental parts of the catching action. The action of catching is offensive in nature. It needs proper understanding and preparation to execute that action. Please remember what I am saying here. The mental understanding is very important for a tennis player. When you see a tennis ball is coming, your frame of mind is in an attacking mode, and you try to get yourself in a position relative to the ball to make another move. You should be in the offensive frame of mind always. With the frame of mind of being there to meet the ball, you will be the pursuer who started the first step. When you see one animal try to catch another animal, it is always the pursuer who started the first step to run after the prey. Once the running action starts, the faster one and the one with better stamina will finally win. To have the mental understanding of getting there is to encourage the pursuer to have an early start. You know, on the tennis court, it is not how fast you can run; it is really how early you start to run to the ball that makes the difference.

The catching we are talking about it here is not a full sport action. It is an action we use to do something after we get to that position. Just like in the African jungle, it is a struggle of life and death. This is true all over the place during prehistoric times.

Since we are talking about the action of catching, we emphasize the ability to run. These actions are related to mammals. We also understand that running is not critically related to the survival of many other animals. There are some animals that have the skills and abilities of body movement to avoid being caught. Jumping into the water, climbing up a tree, and abrupt turning are all survival skills. There are also some animals that possess defensive skills and weapons. They can scare off their pursuers.

We also know that all animals will use what they have and will do what they can to survive. We want the reader to understand that the mental understanding of the concept of catching here is important for us as tennis players today. It is essentially what we are talking about when we play tennis. It is the mental understanding of our footwork. When you play tennis, you have to aggressively get to the ball. Sometimes, the ball is far away from you and you know that it is coming, so why hurry; you will automatically wait for the ball to come. This waiting frame of my mind is what I want you to avoid. Of course, sometimes you may overrun the ball and cannot make a good shot. We have to judge how fast the ball is coming and how early and how fast we have to run. Our eyes will take care of all of these. With more practice, we will have plenty of experience to deal with this problem. However, the sense of aggressively getting to the ball is the mental understanding of the catching action.

Being human, we cannot run as fast as a rabbit or even a dog. Just running to catch prey to survive in a jungle is out of the question even though we have a superior catching mechanism and we have perfect eye-hand coordination. The catching action, though, could not have been the principal mechanism for humans to survive in the prehistoric times. Our running ability is not sufficient to catch large animals in the wildness. We probably only used our running ability to run away from danger. The abilities of hunting and gathering go back to the ability of using our hands to survive prehistorically.

b.   The Action of Hitting

From our understanding of the human hand structure, we know that human hand has a built-in sense of direction of extension. Therefore, a person is able to hold an elongated object such as a stick, a knife, a spear, or any long, sharp object to poke, strike, or swing to hit. The direction of extension of the elongated object a person held is exactly the direction of extension of a person's index finger when the hand is fully extended. This is physiological. We have demonstrated this in a previous section of the human hand structure. The human hand also has a group of powerful fingers to hold these elongated objects. These elongated objects were the weapons people used to fight in wars for thousands of years. Remember, though, the hitting action in the upper-extremity sports such as in tennis, golf, or baseball are not inaccurate motions of swings. There are precise designed, purposeful aimed action. They can cause tremendous damage when a contact is made. This extended, elongated object in the hand of humans is a very powerful weapon. There is no other primate that can do things like this. There is no other primate that can match this kind of physical tribute. The hitting action becomes the most powerful action in the animal kingdom. The weapons can be different; the action of hitting is imprinted in our neurological system. The action of hitting is simple and clear. In a hard hitting, especially, it is also a bulletistic action. That means the power at contact depends on the initial velocity. Since the length of the weapon is limited, if one wants to hit, he has to be close to the object to make the contact. Therefore, we say the action of hitting is a proximal action. I also call it a localized action. It simply means for an action of hitting, it is a more or less a pure rotational motion biomechanically. You do not have to reach out to make the contact. Either it is a flying object that already comes to you or you have already run close enough to make the hit. Also remember that hitting emphasizes on direct contact. Poor contact is poor hitting. No contact is no hitting.

The hitting action has been used as an offensive and defensive action ever since human was existed. There is no other primate that can perform this action with directional control. It is one of humans' primary survival actions. Different weapons can be used to make this action extremely dangerous.

When other animals like dogs, cats, lions, and tigers see a human hold a stick in his hand, they all know what the human can do with that stick. The animals must be very scared. The animals would probably think again and again about what they should and should not do. This is the reason even lion and tiger tamers and other animal trainers always have a little stick in their hand.

Even today, when we have a stick in our hand, we will feel somehow we are protected. For example, if we are going out to take a walk and suddenly, a vicious dog runs at us, if we do not have anything in our hand and we know that we cannot run away from the dog because the dog runs faster than we do, there is no way we can defend ourselves. We will be in great danger. If we have a big stick in our hand, the situation will be the just opposite. The dog probably will run away from us because the dog knows what we can do with that stick. Running away from danger is a common characteristic of all animals. As a human, running away from danger is also human nature. Most wild animals run faster than a human does. It is the first reaction of the human neurological system when in danger. So running is also part of human survival skills.

Since the beginning of human history, humans must coinhabit on this planet with all kinds of animals. Each one strives to survive. Other animals certainly all know what humans could do to survive at that time. The situation between animals (such as lions and tigers) and humans must have something similar to the situation we have today, except the environmental changes and ecological changes.

I must point out that the basic concept that the action of hitting is innate. Some people may be better hitters. Some people may not be as good as others; however, everybody knows how to hit and everybody can hit.

I also have to emphasize again that to execute the action hitting, the mental understanding is here. The object we intended to contact is here. We do not consider what happens to the object except to make the contact here. I call the hitting action a localized action. Because when I make a hitting action, there is nothing more than just hearing "I hit."

When you say here "I hit," you are actually practicing your hitting concentration. You are also using the most important mental parameters: the eye and the mind. These two mental parameters can help each other; they can also interfere with each other. We will discuss them separately later.

Hitting is, no doubt, one principal survival skill of humans. We will postpone the biomechanics of hitting in the later chapter.

c.   The Action of Throwing

The concept of throwing must have originated from the early developmental stage of human beings from the womb. Like any other innate actions, it is the nature of the human race. The throwing action, however, involves the total body's coordinated movements biomechanically. It may also involve basic neurological development of the brain to begin with. These survival actions are innate, not learned. Even though newborn babies do not know how to throw, they will grow into it naturally. So the concept of throwing must have existed in the brain in the developmental stage. Some of the other primates can perform a tossing motion. The tossing motion and the throwing concept are entirely different.

Throwing is an extremely complicated biomechanical action. Mentally it involves a coordinated eye-hand movement. It also involves the sense of trajectory to the target area. Biomechanically it requires the total coordinated rotational body system to perform the mentally prescribed throwing action. The throwing parameters such as releasing point, releasing angle, and the specific type of throwing action (underhand or overhand) will all be considered. This is the most complicated and most difficult total motor program. As humans, we have the capability to figure it out in a matter of second, but it needs practice to make the throwing action perfect. We can tentatively conclude that the throwing program is imprinted in the human neurological system. The basic concept of throwing is to make something "from here to there." With the throwing concept mentally and intellectually being a part of innate human ability, humans are capable of developing and inventing apparatus with the throwing characteristics. This is the reason humans can invent slings and bows and arrows and design guns and all the modern weapon systems. Even the space exploration today is also based on the human innate capability of the throwing concept.

Now let me give you an example: if you ask a person to throw ten tennis balls to a target of ten yards, twenty yards, thirty yards, and fifty yards away, you will find this person will use all the throwing parameters as I discussed in previous paragraph to accomplish his job. He may not be able to perform perfectly as ordered; however, he will make reasonable adjustments of all the mental and biomechanical parameters to carry out this assignment. Even though throwing is an innate action, it still takes a child many years for this action to be fully developed. The first stage of this action is a releasing motion from the hand. Gradually it will develop into an underhanded tossing motion. The finally complete throwing motion will be a full-swing motion with rotation of the body and releasing action of the hand in the direction of the extended index finger and in the same line as the extended arm.

If we do a survey on the earth surface to see if anybody does not know how to make a throw, we will probably find that there is nobody who does not know how to throw. There may be good throwers or bad throwers, but everybody knows how to throw. What does this fact tell us? It simply means that throwing is absolutely human nature.

We all have thrown things many, many times before. We all know how to make a strong throwing motion. Now, if we see a very strong muscular man who holds an object in his hand. He then rotates his hip, turns his shoulder, extends his arm, snaps his wrist, opens his hand, and releases an object and guides the flying object with his index finger and the extended arm. This is a very powerful releasing motion. If we think how fast a baseball pitcher throws a fast ball or how far a football quarterback can throw a football in modern sports, we can understand the power of this throwing action during the prehistoric times in the jungle. We could understand what kind of impact the human made upon different kind of animals.

Just imagine how other animals at that time would have felt when they saw another animal standing there and walking and running on two feet and with two arms swinging wildly with a long stick and hitting everything in sight and, even more dangerously, releasing a rock flying at them. Whenever and wherever a human was present; all you could see was birds flying and animals running away. When any animal saw rocks flying at them like that, the scary feeling was unavoidable.

Even in civilized society today, humans are still using this action in political demonstrations, etc. Explosive tossing and rock throwing are still the common behavior in this violent world. Throwing is a survival skill, and it is also a war fighting skill. If any other animal had any intellectual capability to learn, there is no doubt in my mind they would all know what humans could do from their limited civilized world.

Here, let me mention a personal story. When I was a boy, I grew up in the countryside in the northern part of China. We usually walked miles to school every day. To encounter unfriendly dogs was a very common thing. As I was a young boy, you understand how scared I was then. My father told me one thing that was very valuable. He said, "Son, if you see an unfriendly dog running toward you, do not run away. Pretend to pick up something from the ground—even if there is nothing—to make a throwing motion at the dog, then the dog will slow down or stop and just bark at you." It worked beautifully.

At approximately the same time, there was a rumor that people had seen a wolf in the vicinity too. I remember that was in the summertime, about July or August. My father asked me to hold a stick in my hand when I walked to school. There was a saying then: "The wolf is afraid of the stick, and the dog is afraid of the rock."

Nowadays, whenever we see animal tamers at work, he/she always has a stick in his/her hand. It always reminds me of the things my father told me during my childhood.

Since we are discussing the action of throwing in this section, I like to mention another story, which is even worth thinking about, in my opinion, by children psychologists as a case study.

Many years ago, one day, I went to the post office at the west side of Ann Arbor to mail a package. There was a long line waiting for service. Behind me there was a beautiful young lady pushing a stroller with a very cute little boy in it. That little boy had a pacifier in his mouth, and sometimes it was in his hand to play with. I always liked children. This little boy attracted my attention.

He took the pacifier out of his mouth and played with it, and suddenly, he dropped the pacifier on the ground. He had a big smile on his face. His mother, of course, was not very happy. She picked up the pacifier, cleaned it, and gave it back to the little boy and said, "Johnny, don't drop it. If you drop it again, I will take it away from you." Little John held the pacifier and played with it again. After a minute or so, little John dropped the pacifier again. He was so happy and excited, and he almost laughed. His mother, of course, was not very happy. She picked up that pacifier, cleaned it, and put it inside her purse. The poor little boy was so sad, and he cried and cried.

This young lady seemed sorry that she had made her child cry. In order to justify her own action, she turned to me and said, "I do not know what's happening to my little Johnny these days. He's started dropping things recently. He drops his pacifier. He drops his toys. He even drops fruits and foods when I give him something to eat. It seems the more I ask him not to drop, the more he does it. It is difficult for me to keep his pacifier clean."

I had no knowledge of children psychology. I could only guess from what I knew about how humans work with human hands. I said to her, "Let me make one suggestion, and see if it works. Next time, you give him a ping-pong ball and tell John to drop the ping-pong ball instead of the pacifier. You can even demonstrate to him how you drop the ping-pong ball. If you can demonstrate to him how you drop it and explain to him why you drop the ping-pong ball but not the pacifier, it will be an opportunity for Johnny to learn a few more things at this stage of his age."

Then I tried to explain why I made that suggestion: "Johnny is exploring the world at his age. He is learning new things every day. A child his age, physiologically, is still in the stage of development. For an adult, everybody knows how to toss things and throw things. This toss and throw action is very complicated. It takes two, three years to develop. To open the hand and release something from a person's hand is the first stage of the action of tossing and throwing. When little John drops something from his hand, he thinks he has discovered something new in his life. He is very excited. To him, it is a new discovery. You can see how happy he is. Now you ask him not to drop, he does not know why. Now if you ask him to drop the ping-pong balls, not the pacifier, he will be able to understand something can be dropped and something should not be dropped."

That young lady seemed surprised with my comment. She asked, "Are you a child psychologist?"

I said no.

She kept asking, "How do you know all this?"

I said, "From watching the game of tennis and from my own superficial observation."

She was surprised at what I said, of course. She thanked me sincerely for my suggestion. I did not follow up that story because I was not interested in children psychology, and I did not know how my suggestion turned out.

19

Survival Actions Are Innate Actions

a. All animals have their own survival skills.

Survival skills are actually the things animals do when they need food to survive or during a life-and-death struggle when they encounter their enemy. If any animal does not have any survival skill, there will be no chance for that animal to survive at all.

Birds fly. Fishes swim. Land animals run. All the survival skills are the natural and normal life activities of those animals. All survival skills are innate in that animal's system. All animals practice their survival skills as their exercises.

We often see two animals chase each other playfully. They run after each other playfully. They hide from each other playfully. They wrestle with each other playfully. They bite each other playfully. All these activities are innate to that specific animal.

Animals with superior survival skills survive easier, and animals with inferior survival skills live with difficulties. The animal population in the world today is a strong indication of what animals can do in their survival system.

b. The three survival actions, catching, hitting, and throwing, are specific actions for humans.

It is clear that these are innate actions for humans. There is nobody in any human society that does know how to hit or how to throw. He/she could be a good hitter or a bad hitter, a good thrower or a bad thrower, but the movement of the hitting and throwing actions are there. Therefore, we can definitely conclude that hitting and throwing are innate actions for humans. They are natural actions for humans to perform. These actions are part of the human physiological system.

You have the ability to perform these actions to your own potential. The more you do, the better you are. Now, in terms of athletics, you should know that you are born an athlete. Your potential and accomplishments depend on your genetics and your determination to practice and your mental understanding of the athletic actions involved. Coaches are necessary. The coach's responsibilities are helping you to improve your understanding of the nature of the specific athletic actions and to overcome some of your own mental limitations. You are the limitation of your own potential.

As humans, we do not only perform our own innate survival actions, but we also help other animals perform their survival actions. We have seen many dog owners throwing tennis balls and letting their dog to retrieve the balls. The dog practices its catching skill and running ability. Those are their survival skills, and running and catching are their innate actions; tracing the balls are their exercise. We do similar things for many different animals.

20

How Sports Are
Invented and Developed

a. All Animals Are the Riders of the Train of Time

We do not know what other animals know and think because we do not understand their language. We, however, can discuss from a human's perspective.

Humans survived—more importantly, we know how we survived. There is no documented witness during the prehistoric times. However, we think we know. We know what we are and what we can do at the present time. We should know what we could do historically then. There are so many animals here today. These animals should all be there at ancient times then.

The human is the only animal that has the intellectual ability to think and to learn and knows how to use the hand to protect himself. Other animals may have their own intelligence to know something about themselves, but it is very unlikely they know their history, because they do not have a device like a human hand to record their historical events. Humans should never forget the responsibility they have and the historical roles they should play just because the human knows humans are on the higher ground of the animal ladder. The human should be the proctor and not the destroyer in the history of the animal kingdom.

The invention of sports is another step forward in human intelligence and human civilization. Humans practice their survival skills or their war-fighting skills during their leisure times, which became the origin of sports today. If we look at many games people have played historically—in the ancient times, in the countryside, or in the royal palaces—they were all in the nature of the survival actions. The wars in human history were fought in years numbering thousands. The pictures of using the skills hitting, running, and throwing to fight in wars are still vividly in our minds.

b. Industrial Revolution

Progress in civilization, human intelligence, and human ingenuity changed the world. The survival skills humans used only a few thousand years ago were seldom used for survival anymore. We all understand that the survival skills are primarily the skills to save people's lives. They are all primarily fighting skills during the war to fence external aggressions. During the prehistoric time, no matter what kinds of weapons people used, people always used arm swing, hitting, and throwing skills to fight in the war. After the Industrial Revolution, those old-fashioned weapons did not work anymore. Ammunitions, firearms, guns, and cannons all become fight tools, and the old fighting skills also were not useful anymore. People, however, still retained those skills they were born with, so humans—unconsciously or deliberately—used their innate skills as their exercise. This way, the sports activities gradually emerged as the modern sports. New sports were invented. Old skills were modified. Major sports and recreation sports all emerged as part of the normal development of our human activity. All these activities are part of our human nature. They are part of our human system. When we do them, we feel good.

c. Modern Sport Actions

All the modern sports today are derived from the different games people played historically through the ages. They are basically designed to practice the human survival skills of running, catching, hitting, throwing, and kicking. Of course, there are other sport activities such as horse riding and archery and many other minor sports activities.

We are only interested in the major survival-related human physical activities in this book.

As we have mentioned, the human is the rider of the train of time. People can think and look ahead, but they cannot live ahead of their time. People can only enjoy what they have and accomplish with what they can at their time and age. Time is the limiting factor. Format of the game, rules of the game, equipment of the game—everything changes with time. So early games and modern games must be very different. Even though the games are different, the actions in the game should be very similar, since the sports activities are part of human nature. When people perform those activities, they feel comfortable. Also, because the human instinct of survival is extremely strong, survival activity can become very serious and very competitive. Sports activities are always going to be very popular in any society.

I am going to discuss the most critical aspect of several games in the following sections. The important thing to discuss about sports is to discuss about the athletic actions, just like we have discussed so far. From our understanding of the human hand structure, our understanding of the relationship of our hands and our neurological system, to our understanding of the athletic terms we are using today and using the athletic actions, these are the best ways to explain athletic events. Therefore, we use the action of catching, the action of hitting, and the action of throwing to discuss all the athletic events.

21

The Concept of Balance

a.   Humans have an ideal balance system

I've heard so many sport coaches so often mention the word *balance*. They often criticize their players for not having good balance and let them practice balance, especially the tennis coaches.

Probably it is the best time now to talk about the concept of balance. The human being has the most sophisticated and perfect balancing mechanism among all the bipedal animals. Human balance is controlled neurologically through our ear canal. It is something we do automatically and do not have to know. If we do not have good balance, we would not even be able to stand up. Once a person stands up straight, any movement of his body is balanced by the relative movement of another part of his body. In the human system, except the trunk system, there is the head on the top, and there are the limb systems on both sides of the trunk. The limb system and the head can produce unbalance of the whole body. This overall unbalance can be balanced by moving the relative limb and the hip motion to produce a balanced weight distribution.

The advantage of the human balance system statically over any other primates depends on the left-right, up-down, and especially the movable middle hip base to keep a static balance of the human body. All these features are based on the free movement of the shoulder joints on the top and the ball-and-socket hip joints in the middle of the trunk system.

The special feature of the moving human system is to keep the balance in the middle of the human body. During the human movement, the left arm is synchronized with the right leg, and the right arm is synchronized with the left leg. Human walking and running is a left-and-right mini rotational motion and rotation about the base of the trunk. It is very important to understand that human athletic movements are basically rotational in nature. To define the center of rotation is the first step to define the proper athletic action.

b. Athletic unbalance is caused by improper execution of athletic actions. Unbalance in athletics is a mental problem.

I often see many tennis players running, jumping, and working with very fancy steps; they all say that they are practicing balance. When I see their coaches are seriously overseeing the player's activities, I became speechless. It is apparent that there are so many misconceptions in the game of tennis or sports in general about the problems of balance. Even coaches do not understand the problems of balance and unbalance in sports and are less than able to help their players to solve the problem.

Human body is a total stepwise rotational system. The execution of any athletic action with the human body is also rotational in nature. Ideally speaking, it is very easy for humans to perform rotational action. However, in an athletic performance, athletes tend to have extra unnecessary thoughts, such as "I want to hit hard" during a golf swing, or "I want to hit the ball there" in a tennis swing. All these extra thoughts tend to modify the natural swing pattern of human body rotation. This is the reason I said that unbalance is a mental problem.

It is true that unbalance in athletic performance is a serious problem. However, practicing the well-defined proper athletic actions are the only ways to prevent unbalance. Do not inject any unnecessary thought into your normal practice swing.

22

Some Modern Sports

a. Baseball

In baseball, the batters hit. The catchers catch. The outfielders catch and throw. The pitchers throw. Every player has his own assignment, and every player plays his own role.

An important thing I have to mention here is that the nature of the athletic action has to be understood precisely by the players and the coaches. Every action has its own physical and mental parameters. Physical parameters are responsible for how fast a person can run, how hard a person can hit, and how strong a person can perform. Mental parameters are related to how precise the players can perform and that they do not make unnecessary unforced errors. If the player wants to be a great player and the coach wants to be a good coach, understanding these parameters clearly is the only way to help the players to play and to help the coaches to coach. Of course, every game has its special strategy; however, strategy is only secondary to the primary physical and mental understanding of the athletic actions and the concentration to perform them.

A player performing the action the closest to its mental and physical conditions will become the best player in whatever he is doing. Here, I am not going into detail of the biomechanical part of the actions; I am emphasizing on the mental aspect of the actions specifically.

Now, let's us to reiterate the basic concept of the actions different players are facing and point out the possible mental interferences affecting the performance of those actions.

For Baseball Pitchers

Throwing is the most important athletic action in baseball. All baseball players are good throwers. The throwing action requires strength and precision. Baseball pitchers are the most accurate throwers. I think many baseball players can throw the ball harder and faster than a lot of pitchers. The reason baseball players and outfielders are not pitchers is simply because they have played their position for a long time and they are good at that position. Players playing in different positions think differently. What one player thinks is one of the most important mental factors in any mental training program. They were never trained for pitching positions in their career. With a good pitching coach and a sound mental training program, many baseball players can be trained to be good pitchers.

Good baseball pitching requires power and precision. Precision is the most important factor. Pitching is using a series of dynamic segments of the body to produce a fast-moving rotation. This is a total coordinated lower- and upper-body rotational system. If we use a horse and carriage as an example, the lower body is the horse and the upper extremity is the carriage. If you want to throw as fast as you can, you use the lower extremity and your trunk to build up as much potential energy as possible for your arm to make a final delivery. The main idea is for the lower body to wind up and delay the arm's forward motion until the last second. The principal rotation centers are critical. For a right-hand thrower, the rotational centers are the left hip and the right shoulder. The combination of these joints determines the power and the precision of the delivery. The general principle is the following: if the performing member is on the right side of the body, the left side is the helping member; if the performing member is on the upper part of the body, the lower part of the body is the helping member, and vice versa. The old cliché says, "Never get your carriage ahead of the horse." Here, the performing member is the carriage and the helping member is the horse.

In the action of pitching here, the releasing of the hand is the carriage and the turning of the body is the horse. The possible interference here is at the releasing point; the pitcher should avoid having any part of the body interfere with the releasing action, especially the head's or the eyes' unnecessary movement. This is the important part of the precession of the pitching action. This is the *mental* part of the pitching action.

Now let us repeat it. The power portion of the pitching comes from the rotation of the hip and the delayed internal rotation of the shoulder, and the precision comes from the movement of the elbow and snap of the wrist. The wrist is the final directly performing member of the throwing system. The *mental* part of the throwing should be concentrated on the last releasing motion. The thumb and the middle finger firmly control the ball, and the index finger guides the direction of releasing. The hand has an independent accelerating and releasing mechanism. The whole throwing and releasing mechanism is guided and lead by the eye. It is a close eye-hand cooperation process. Action is like a blind person, and the eye is like a leader dog of the blind. The hand will use its own accelerating mechanism (snapping the wrist) to release the ball or an object at a specific point and time during the swing motion. This is a preprogrammed total body motion.

The most important thing for a pitcher when pitching is not trying too hard to see the target area. It is better to think about the releasing with the eye to see the target area. If you focus too hard on the target area, your releasing motion will be compromised. It is very important not to use your head to help you in the releasing motion. Whatever you do, the action itself is the most important factor to think about. The action is restricted to the movement of the link system. When you throw a ball, the arm (from the shoulder joint to the tip of the finger) is the total performing unit and the hand is the direct performing member. So, snap of the wrist and release the ball from the opening of the index finger is the last movement of the throwing action. Therefore, the wrist and the hand are the direct performing members that should be on a pitcher's mind at the time of release; the elbow and the shoulder joints are the primary power providers and helping members. Maintaining a steady head position during releasing motion is very important in a throwing action. If we use the horse and the carriage as examples to think about the throwing motion, the movement of the lower extremity to prepare your upper trunk is the horse and the arm from the shoulder down to the hand is the carriage. The throwing power will be there if you do not let the carriage run ahead of the horse.

For Baseball Batters

All baseball players are terrific hitters. This is a typical static hitting with an incoming flying object. That means the batter stands still and sees a coming flying subject; you then make a swing with an implement to make a contact. This is a typical hitting action. As humans, anybody can make a hit. A person with good athletic ability will make contact without much difficulty. A person with less adequate athletic ability will miss the contact. However, with enough practice, anybody can become a decent hitter. The ability to make contact is a pure athletic problem. The mental problem is not serious if the hatter just thinks about contact and does not think too much about other things.

The mental factors will come in when the level of physical condition rises to the level of baseball games. When the ball comes in faster and faster, it is more difficult for the batter to make an ideal contact if the batter does not understand what is the best way to think and to understand how to use his eyes to watch the ball.

How to see the ball depends on what is on your mind. To see and to think are mental. They interfere with each other unless you think and see the same thing. The relation between the mind and eye is a very interesting one. This is a very important subject in almost all the athletic performances. The eye function is a very important part of the mind function. The eyes collect all the information for our minds to make a decision to react. In general, what we want to do is preplanned. For example, you see something you hit if it is a hitting program, or you see something you catch if it is a catching program. All these programs are all preprogrammed in our neurological system, just like when we assign a person to play pitcher, batter, or outfielder. However, if something happens suddenly and it is not preplanned, then your eye will automatically activate your defensive system to do whatever is necessary to protect yourself.

A baseball batter tries to hit a ball. He even plans to hit a certain way. This is his mind at work. When he stands on the plate to hit, suddenly a wild pitch, a ball flying fast, approaches him. He either tries to dodge the ball or tries to use something to block the ball. This is his eye at work. In general, the eyes collect the information and let the mind make the decision. However, during an emergency situation, there is no time for the mind to make any decision, and the eyes will take over to make the decision. That means in the reflex arc neurologically, a certain reaction does not have to go all the way to the decision-making portion of the brain.

In our human system, even though our brain is incomparable, it takes time for our system to work. For neurological signals to travel, it requires time. For our eyes to move, it requires time. A decision requires time. Therefore, in order to see things efficiently, one must relax the eyes to begin with, especially to see a fast-moving object.

Here, we also have to differentiate the concept of seeing and focusing. Using the word *see* is more proper than using the word *focus*. To focus is too strong for us to see a fast-moving object. If we focus on a fast-moving object too strongly, we are always going to be late to react to the moving object because of the retention time of the eyes. This is the limitation of our eyes. This is the reason we see a movie as a continuous picture and not slide by slide. We have to relax our eyes in order to see the fast-moving objects better. Therefore, for a baseball better, it is necessary to relax the eye function. It is also very important for a base batter not to think of anything when he is ready to make a hit. Just think of meeting the ball or of catching the ball with your bat with a comfortable swing.

Baseball Outfielders

For people who play base or outfield, their main job is to catch and throw. Catching and throwing is a compound action, or you can call it a double action. As I mentioned earlier about the compound action, the second action is always an interference of the first action. You can never think about throw the ball before you are sure that you have the ball in your hand.

We often see a football player thinking about running and missing his catch. This thing happens in baseball games too. Even though it does not happen too often in pro games, it can happen if the proper concentration is not there.

According to the concentration mechanism, the first concentration is on the catching. For the flying balls, the catchers have to run to the ball as fast as possible, but the velocity of the flying ball is not that great; the word *focus* is the eyes' function to execute. To track the ball as focused as possible until the contact is made then to execute the throwing action. Of course, you want to throw as early as possible, but you have to realize that the intention to throw is the most serious interference factor for your catching action. Once they catch the ball, throwing is not a problem for most outfielders.

b. Tennis

The modern tennis game we are playing today is a little over one hundred years old. It was probably modified from similar games people played through the ages. It is basically the product of biological progression. The availability of the material making the ball and the availability of the material making the racket must be very different in different stages of the development. However, the physical actions involved in playing the game should be very similar. The tennis actions, catching, hitting, and throwing, are a series of more complicated athletic actions. These are the actions we have talked about previously again and again. These actions are the human survival skills. These are the innate actions of the human race. These are the actions people do or did in exercise. These are the actions people used in wars before the modern weapons were invented. These actions are parts of normal human activities. These are the actions of common physical exercises. Once you do it, you feel comfortable.

People used to say that tennis is a game of a lifetime. Yes, it is true. I have friends who still played tennis after they passed ninety. By the way, I would also like to recommend people to take up the game of golf. I have known a friend who played golf when he passed the age of one hundred.

I have stressed this previously—that tennis is one of the most complete action sports nowadays. It is much easier than the other complete sport, hockey. It is much easier to run or walk on the ground than skate on the ice.

We have also stressed that one simple tennis stroke contains all the sports action in a whole base game. I remember many years ago when my children were growing up. My older son, Gary, came home from one of his Little League baseball games with a long face. I asked him what was wrong. He said, "I did not get a chance to hit." There had been so many kids that day. He did get a chance to play on the field, but he did not get a chance to bat. Catching, hitting, and throwing are the series of human survival actions; you have a sense of completion if you can do all these actions. This is the reason I say tennis is one of the most complete action sports.

Usually when people watch tennis matches or when coaches watch their students play among themselves, they sit by the courtside and watch the ball fly across the net. They turn their head—left, right, left, right, left, right, left, right. Finally, when one mistake is made, the player will often blame himself or look at his racket and feel this racket is lousy. Even worse, many children, whenever an unforced error is made, smash their rackets on the ground and yell, "You're stupid! Grandma can do it!" They swear at themselves and end up with a smashed racket. All these children are not stupid at all. Actually, they are just too smart. They think too much of the things they should not think about at all; they miss the very simple things they should think about. Their intellectual abilities make them think much more than what they should think about—the simple actions. They complicate the game tremendously. That is the reason I specially point out the intellectual interference. Without understanding the source of the interference, they could never concentrate to the degree they should to play the game. All these factors drive me into a field I am not trained for.

Tennis players are probably the athletes that take more private lessons than most other athletes. I am not against students taking private lessons. I like to see a student learn something very specifically in each lesson. I favor a student who practices what he has learned at least one hour after he has learned it. There are so many things a developing tennis player should be learning. If he learns without practicing on his own, he does not learn. Actually, almost everything a student learns is an important part of the *mental* game of tennis. We have often heard people say, "Tennis is all mental." However, nobody has ever defined what *mental tennis* is. Now, let me try to define mental tennis.

The definition of *mental game* I have given is the following: Mental tennis, in my mind, is (1) what you think in your mind, (2) what you know, (3) how you feel, (4) what you see and how you see, and (5) what you do and how you do. It sounds so complicated; actually, it is not, because all the things we should know are only associated with the three athletic actions. For every action, there are just a few specific mental and biomechanical parameters. Tennis players only do one action at one time. There are not many things you have to know and to think to execute that simple action. Anything other than proper execution of that action is an interference factor.

Those who engage in sports education should understand the importance of the total training process. Teaching your student to understand the game is the most important part of the teaching program in my mind. Students should have self-appreciation of the game. Students should think and rethink what the coaches taught them and find time to practice themselves without their coaches' presence. Eventually, when the students play in a match or in practice, they should know exactly why or how a mistake happened. To be able to correct themselves is the essence of why people take lessons. Even though the tennis game is more complicated than other games, once we understand it, it is a very simple, enjoyable game.

The best way to understand the game is to compare it with a baseball game. In baseball, every player has a role to play. Catchers catch, pitchers throw, batters hit, and outfielders catch and throw. Of course, every baseball player needs to run and run well. Without proper lower body support, there is nothing that can be done.

What are the actions in tennis we are talking about then? When you are playing tennis, if you see a ball is coming, first, you have to run to meet the ball. This action is just like any outfielder in baseball running to catch a flying ball. This running toward the ball is a catching action. The most efficient way to get there is to have maximum concentration in catching. I have mentioned this before—the maximum catching concentration is to think "get there" and nothing else, because anything else other than "get there" will not help you to get there. Furthermore, anything else other than "get there" will interfere with you getting there.

There is another very important concept I have to mention here; that is, for every athletic action, there is a pre-action. This pre-action could be mental or physical, but it is not the action itself. For example, a player always has something on his mind before he needs to do something. This can be classified as a pre-action thought. This is not the action thought, but it is related to the action. For example, the defensiveness or offensiveness are pre-action thoughts. This mental state can be classified as a pre-action state. Another example—if you want to swing forward with your racket, you have to have your racket back to begin with. The back swing can be classified as a pre-action of the forward swing action. This back swing can be classified as physical pre-action.

When an outfielder in the baseball game waits on the field to catch a flying ball, before the ball comes, he can think aggressively to attack the flying ball or he can think to wait for the ball coming. This is pre-action mental state.

In a tennis match, one player prepares to receive a serve from his/her opponent. He/she jumps up and down to prepare to attack the incoming ball, or he thinks and waits to see where the ball is going. This is also pre-action mental state.

In both cases, the players know themselves whether they are in a defensive state or in an offensive mental state. It is important that in tennis, the player has to be in an aggressive or offensive mental state to execute the *catching* action.

When a lion hides in the grass watching a deer eating the grass some distance away, the lion is preparing to make a move at the deer. The lion, with a slight movement of its paw, is preparing to make a first jump.

This attacking mode is an activation factor for the action of catching. This offensive frame of mind is very important in the catching action in tennis. With this attacking mode, the player may be able to start his running motion one step or half a step earlier. On the tennis court, it is not how fast a player can run; it is how early a player can start running. One step or half a step is enough to make a play or fail in a play. This is a very important part of the mental game of catching action. The concept of "go to attack the incoming ball" is the pre-action of the catching action. This is mental. It is very important to the concentration of the catching action in tennis. Here, I have to emphasize the concept that the idea of attacking the ball is not for the action of hitting. It is for the player to aggressively get to the ball. Once the player gets within the distance to make the contact, the concentration already changes from the catching mode to a hitting mode. For an outfield, it is to contact the ball with eye-hand coordination to make a catch. For a tennis player, the concentration changes from a catching mode to a hitting concentration and to make a swing to contact the ball.

THE DIFFERENCE OF TENNIS FROM OTHER SPORTS COMES FROM THE FOLLOWING DISCUSSION. I WANT TO DESCRIBE IT WITH CAPITAL LETTERS. I HOPE ALL TENNIS PLAYERS, TENNIS PARENTS, TENNIS COACHES, AND ALL TENNIS LOVERS STUDY THIS SECTION SERIOUSLY AND CAREFULLY. ESPECIALLY FOR COACHES, IF YOU UNDERSTAND THIS SECTION THOROUGHLY AND CLEARLY, IT WILL HELP YOU TO UNDERSTAND THE GAME FROM INSIDE OUT, AND IT WILL ALSO HELP YOU TO COACH ANY OTHER SPORT IF YOU ARE INTERESTED. I AM ALSO GOING TO REITERATE AGAIN AND AGAIN MANY POINTS RELATED TO THE NATURE OF THE GAME AND THE NATURE OF THE HUMAN SYSTEM. FIRST, I WANT TO SAY IT AGAIN: TO BEGIN WITH, A HUMAN IS BORN TO PERFORM THE ACTIONS OF CATCHING, HITTING, AND THROWING. THESE ACTIONS ARE THE BASIC SURVIVAL SKILLS FOR HUMANS DURING THE PREHISTORIC TIMES. THESE SURVIVAL SKILLS ARE THE PRESENT-DAY SPORTS

SKILLS. EVERYBODY IS BORN AN ATHLETE. EVERYBODY HAS HIS OWN ATHLETIC POTENTIAL.

WHEN A TENNIS PLAYER SWINGS HIS/HER RACKET FAST AND FOCUSES ONLY ON MAKING CONTACT WITH THE BALL, HE/SHE PERFORMS AN ACTION OF HITTING. HE ALSO WISHES THE BALL TO FLY OVER THE NET AND LAND IN A SPECIFIC AREA, AND HIS OPPONENT CANNOT GET THERE TO MAKE THE RETURN. THIS TENNIS PLAYER USES THE ACTION OF HITTING TO ACCOMPLISH A JOB, WHICH, BASICALLY, IS LIKE A THROWING JOB. THIS TENNIS PLAYER MAY THINK THAT HE MADE A GOOD HIT. HOWEVER, IF A TENNIS PLAYER MAKES A GOOD LOB OVER THE HEAD OF HIS/HER OPPONENT AND HIS OPPONENT CANNOT RETURN HIS/HER LOB, THIS PLAYER MAY FEEL HE MADE A GOOD THROW. IN ESSENCE, A HIT IS A HIT, AND A LOB IS LIKE A THROW. YOU CAN ALSO CALL THE LOB A SOFT HIT. DIFFERENT PEOPLE MAY THINK DIFFERENTLY. IT IS ALL IN PEOPLE'S MINDS.

HOWEVER, IN OUR CASE, WE DEFINE THE HIT AS USING THE RACKET TO CONTACT THE BALL, AND THE BALL IS NOT RELEASED FROM THE HAND. SO A HARD HIT IS A HIT, AND A SOFT HIT IS ALSO A HIT.

THE DIFFERENCE BETWEEN HIT AND THROW COMES FROM THE HAND'S FUNCTION. IN A HITTING MOTION, THE HAND IS CLOSED. THE MOTION IS DRAWING IN OVERALL. IN A THROWING ACTION, THE HAND IS OPEN. THERE IS AN ACTION OF RELEASING. THE SENSE OF EXTENSION IS THE TOTAL BODY MOTION. EXCEPT FOR THE HAND MOTION, THE REST OF THE BODY'S MOTION LOOKS VERY SIMILAR. IN THESE TWO PHYSICAL ACTIONS, HITTING AND THROWING, THE WAYS OF SWINGING THE RACKET LOOK ALMOST THE SAME EXCEPT THE HAND, BUT THE WAY THEY THINK AND HOW THEY USE THEIR EYES TO SEE ARE VERY DIFFERENT. SO WE CAN SEE THAT THE TENNIS GAME IS INVENTED IN SUCH A WAY THAT

THERE IS A HIDDEN TRAP IN THE GAME. WHEN YOU HIT THE BALL, THE OVERALL GOAL IS TO MAKE THE BALL GO OVER THE NET AND LAND AT THE OTHER SIDE OF THE COURT. WHEN A TENNIS PLAYER USES A HITTING ACTION TO PERFORM A JOB, WHICH IS BASICALLY THROWING IN NATURE, IT IS ALMOST LIKE YOU ARE USING A HITTING SOFTWARE PROGRAM IN A COMPUTER AND YOU WANT TO SEE A RESULT AS A THROWING ACTION. AS HUMANS, WE CAN DO IT. HOWEVER, WE DO NOT DO IT WITHOUT ANY DIFFICULTIES. THIS IS THE REASON I AM WRITING. THIS IS THE REASON SO MANY PEOPLE GET FRUSTRATED WHEN PLAYING TENNIS. WHEN THE PLAYER IS HITTING SOMETHING, THE ACTION IS TAKING PLACE LOCALLY. IT IS HERE. THE THING HE IS GOING TO HIT IS RIGHT IN FRONT OF HIS EYES. WHAT HAPPENS TO THE OBJECT HE IS GOING TO HIT DOES NOT CONCERN HIM AFTER HIS SWING. ALL HE HAS TO DO IS WIND HIS BODY TO MAKE THE SWING. HIS EYES AND HIS MIND ARE SYNCHRONIZED AT THE TARGET AREA TO BE CONTACTED. WHEN WE PLAY TENNIS, WE COMPLICATE THE MATTER TOO MUCH. FIRST, WE SEE THE BALL. IT IS A MOVING TARGET. WE HAVE TO ADJUST OUR POSITION TO MEET THE BALL. WE DO NOT THINK IT IS A SIMPLE CATCHING ACTION. ONCE WE GET THERE AND ARE READY TO MAKE THE SWING, WE HAVE ALREADY THOUGHT OF WHERE WE WISH THE BALL TO GO. SO HITTING A TENNIS BALL IS NOT THAT SIMPLE HIT ANYMORE, ESPECIALLY WHEN WE WANT THE BALL TO FLY TO A CERTAIN AREA. THE MIND IS THINKING. THE EYES ARE WATCHING. THE ARM IS SWINGING. EVEN WE THINK WE ARE IN GOOD CONCENTRATION, BUT WE DO NOT EVEN KNOW WHAT CONCENTRATION REALLY MEANS ANYMORE.

WE HAVE TO REALLY SIMPLIFY OUR CONCEPT OF PLAYING TENNIS TO THE SPECIFIC ACTIONS WE DO. WE KNOW CONCENTRATION IS ACTION SPECIFIC. ONE ACTION HAS ONE CONCENTRATION. IF WE WANT TO CONCENTRATE, WE HAVE TO KNOW WHAT INTERFERENCE. GETTING

RID OF THE INTERFERENCES IS THE ESSENCE OF CONCENTRATION.

WE HAVE MENTIONED PREVIOUSLY SEVERAL TIMES THAT HUMANS ARE BORN TO CATCH, HIT, AND THROW. THESE ACTIONS ARE BASIC HUMAN SURVIVAL SKILLS. THESE ACTIONS ARE INGRAINED IN THE HUMAN NEUROLOGICAL SYSTEM. THE HUMAN BODY IS STRUCTURED BIOMECHANICALLY TO PERFORM THESE ACTIONS. IF WE JUST CONSIDER THESE ACTIONS AND THE PARAMETERS OF THESE ACTIONS, IT WILL BE MUCH EASIER TO FIGURE OUT HOW TO CONCENTRATE TO PERFORM THESE ACTIONS. WE SEE PEOPLE RUN, WE SEE PEOPLE WALK, WE SEE PEOPLE JUMP, AND WE SEE PEOPLE PLAY ALL KINDS OF SPORTS. NO MATTER WHAT SPORT THEY PLAY, THE ACTIONS ARE THE SAME. THE LOWER ATHLETIC SYSTEM (FROM THE HIP DOWN) INVOLVES CATCHING, KICKING, AND JUMPING. THE UPPER ATHLETIC SYSTEM INVOLVES CATCHING, HITTING, AND THROWING. THESE TWO ATHLETIC SYSTEMS STRING TOGETHER AS THE HUMAN ATHLETIC SYSTEM. THE UPPER BODY AND THE LOWER BODY WORK TOGETHER SEAMLESSLY AS A UNIT; NO PART OF THE ATHLETIC ACTIVITY IS INDEPENDENT. WHEN PEOPLE PERFORM THESE ACTIONS, THEY FEEL COMFORTABLE PHYSICALLY. THEY EVEN FEEL GOOD PSYCHOLOGICALLY.

THE ACTIONS OF HITTING AND THROWING SEPARATE HUMANS FROM ALL OTHER PRIMATES. ANY ACTION INVOLVING EYES AND HANDS REQUIRES US TO PAY SPECIAL ATTENTION. AN EYE-AND-HAND PAIRING INVOLVES EYE-HAND COORDINATION OR THE EYE-HAND COOPERATION PROCESS.

LET ME POINT IT OUT NOW: WE HAVE ALREADY FOUND THAT THE TWO ACTIONS, HITTING AND THROWING, HAVE VERY DIFFERENT PARAMETERS BIOMECHANICALLY AND MENTALLY. TWO DIFFERENT ACTIONS TOGETHER

MAY CREATE ACTION-ACTION INTERFERENCE. YES, IT IS TRUE IN THE GAME OF TENNIS. THE TWO ACTIONS ARE NOT JUST TOO CLOSE; THEY ARE ALMOST COMPLETELY MIXED UP.

FOR THE ACTION OF HITTING, THE PHYSICAL PORTION OF THE SWING IS JUST LIKE THAT OF A BLIND PERSON; THE EYE IS LIKE THE LEADER DOG OF THE BLIND. IF YOU THINK ABOUT THE ACTION OF HITTING, THE EYE WILL LEAD YOU TO THE POSITION WHERE YOU CAN SWING YOUR RACKET TO CONTACT THE BALL. THE SWING IS PHYSICAL, AND WHAT YOU THINK AND WHAT YOU SEE IS MENTAL. IF YOU JUST THINK ABOUT CONTACTING THE BALL WITH YOUR SWING AND JUST SEE YOUR CONTACT WITH THE BALL, YOU HAVE PERFECT CONCENTRATION IN YOUR HITTING. IF YOU THINK ABOUT WHERE YOU WANT THE BALL TO GO, THEN YOUR EYES WILL FOLLOW THE BALL. ONCE YOUR EYES MOVE, YOUR SWING MOTION WILL BE INTERRUPTED. WE OFTEN HEAR THE TENNIS COACHES ASK THEIR STUDENT TO KEEP THEIR HEAD STILL. ACTUALLY, IT IS NOT THEIR HEAD. IT IS THEIR EYES, SINCE THE EYES ARE PART OF THE HEAD. WHEN YOUR EYES MOVE THE HEAD HAS TO MOVE. ONCE THE EYES MOVE, THE ACTION OF HITTING TAILED OFF BECOMES PART OF THE THROWING ACTION. IT IS VERY DIFFICULT TO KEEP YOUR EYES AT THE POINT OF CONTACT UNTIL YOU FINISH YOUR SWING COMPLETELY. THIS IS ALSO OUR INTELLECTUAL ABILITY. HOWEVER, WE ARE SMARTER THAN THAT; WE CAN FIGURE OUT THE REAL CONCENTRATION.

JUST AS WE ALREADY MENTIONED, THE EYE TENDS TO LEAD THE ACTION OF WHATEVER WE ARE DOING. WHENEVER YOU WANT TO HIT A BALL TO SOMEWHERE ON THE COURT, YOUR MIND HAS ALREADY COMPLETED THE PLAN AND ORDERS YOUR ATHLETIC SYSTEM TO CARRY OUT THIS PROGRAM. HOWEVER, YOUR EYE STILL LIKES TO KNOW WHERE THE BALL IS GOING. THIS IS

STILL A PART OF OUR OWN INTELLECTUAL ABILITY. THIS
IS WHAT YOU ARE BORN WITH. THIS IS WHAT WE ARE
BORN FOR. THIS IS THE NATURAL WAY THE HUMAN
SYSTEM WORKS. IF WE DO THIS NATURALLY, WE CAN
SAY IT IS THE EYE THAT INTERFERES IN THE ACTION
OF HITTING. IN ORDER TO AVOID THIS INTERFERENCE,
THE ONLY WAY IS TO HAVE A STRONG MIND AND THINK
DECISIVELY: I JUST WANT TO SWING AND KEEP MY EYES AT
THE POINT OF CONTACT. YES, WE CAN DO THIS BECAUSE
THE MIND IS THE ONLY THING THAT CAN CONTROL THE
EYES. ACTUALLY, THIS IS THE REAL MENTAL TOUGHNESS.

THE DEFINITION OF HITTING IS FOR US TO JUST SWING
AT THE TARGET AND KEEP OUR EYES AT THE POINT
OF CONTACT. WE CAN HIT LIGHT; WE CAN HIT HARD.
WHERE THE OBJECT GOES AFTER BEING HIT IS NOT IN
OUR CONSIDERATION. IT IS DIFFERENT FOR US TO HIT
A BALL BECAUSE WHERE THE BALL IS GOING BECOMES
PART OF THE HITTING PROGRAM. IT TAKES A LONG,
LONG TIME FOR ANY GOOD TENNIS PLAYER TO RETAIN
HIS GOOD HITTING SWING MOTION ALL THE TIME
WHEN HE PLAYS TENNIS. EVEN THE BEST TENNIS PLAYER,
UNDER A PRESSURE SITUATION, STILL MAKES MISTAKES
WHEN HE THINKS TOO STRONGLY WHERE HE WANTS
THE BALL TO GO AND OVERLOOKS HIS SWING MOTION.
THIS CONFLICT OF THE ACTION OF HITTING WITH THE
CONCEPT OF THROWING ALL COMES FROM YOUR OWN
INTELLECTUAL ABILITY. THAT IS WHY I CALL THIS KIND
OF INTERFERENCE "INTELLECTUAL INTERFERENCES."

IT IS EXTREMELY DIFFICULT TO CONCENTRATE ON THE
HITTING MECHANISM WITHOUT ANY INTERFERENCE
OF THE CONCEPT OF THE BALL'S MOVEMENT. THE
RESULT OF THIS INTERFERENCE IS WHEN YOU SWING
AT THE BALL, YOU KNOW AND YOU WISH WHERE YOU
WANT THE BALL TO GO. YOUR EYES ARE PROGRAMMED
TO SEE WHERE THE BALL IS GOING. THE ONLY WAY TO
CONTROL YOUR EYES IS FOR YOU TO THINK STRONGLY, "I

JUST WANT TO KEEP MY EYES AT THE POINT OF CONTACT AND NOT MOVE AT ALL." AS WE MENTIONED BEFORE, EYE MOVEMENT IS LIKE CHANGING THE SOFTWARE PROGRAM IN A COMPUTER. ONCE YOU MOVE YOUR EYES, YOUR ORIGINAL PROGRAM OF A HITTING MOTION IS CHANGED.

SO THE TENNIS GAME WAS INVENTED IN SUCH A WAY THAT THERE IS A BUILT-IN MENTAL TRAP TO CONFUSE US WHEN WE USE AN ACTION OF HITTING TO PERFORM A JOB THAT IS BASICALLY THROWING IN NATURE. AS HUMANS, WE HAVE THE INTELLIGENCE AND ABILITY TO MAKE SOME DEGREE OF ADJUSTMENT. THE ADJUSTMENT IS IN THE WAY WE THINK ABOUT OUR SWING. THIS ADJUSTMENT CAN BE SHOWN IN OUR EYE MOVEMENT AND OUR BODY MOVEMENT.

WHY DO COACHES ALWAYS YELL AT THEIR STUDENTS, "KEEP YOUR EYES ON THE BALL"? NOW WE UNDERSTAND WHY TENNIS PLAYERS HAVE TROUBLE KEEPING THEIR EYES ON THE BALL WHEN THEY SWING THEIR RACKETS. FOR THESE TWO ACTIONS, WE "THINK" DIFFERENTLY AND WE USE OUR EYES DIFFERENTLY.

ALL OUR DISCUSSIONS HERE ARE BASICALLY MENTAL IN NATURE. THE CLICHÉ "TENNIS IS ALL MENTAL" SHOWS WHY. THE MIXED NATURE OF HITTING AND THROWING CAN CAUSE SERIOUS PROBLEMS FOR THE MAJORITY OF TENNIS PLAYERS ON ALL LEVELS.

SINCE HITTING AND THROWING ARE BIOMECHANICALLY IDENTICAL, ONLY MENTALLY DIFFERENT, ONE CAN DO THINGS TO MAKE LIGHT CONTACT WITH A HITTING MOTION. YOU CAN ACCOMPANY THIS HITTING MOTION WITH A THROWING THOUGHT. WHEN YOU THROW, YOU HAVE A TRAJECTORY ON YOUR MIND. WHEN YOU HIT, YOU HAVE THE SENSE OF CONTACT ON YOUR MIND. IF YOU MAKE A LOB STROKE IN YOUR GAME, YOU CAN

ACCOMPLISH THIS WITH EITHER A HITTING THOUGHT OR A THROWING THOUGHT. THESE MIXED-UP CONDITIONS CREATE TREMENDOUS CONFUSION IN THE TENNIS TEACHING INDUSTRY. MANY TEACHING PROFESSIONALS USE THE THROWING CONCEPT TO TEACH; MANY TEACHING PROFESSIONALS USE THE HITTING CONCEPT TO TEACH. ACTUALLY, NEITHER GROUP KNOWS EXACTLY WHAT IS REALLY GOING ON.

I THINK IT IS NECESSARY FOR ME TO CLEAR UP THIS CONFUSION. SINCE THE HITTING ACTION REQUIRES THE CRITICAL CONCEPT OF CONTACT, AND ALSO, IT IS THE PRIMARY ACTION IN THE HITTING-THROWING COMPOUND ACTION SERIES, THEREFORE, THE HITTING CONCEPT SHOULD BE GIVEN THE PRIMARY ATTENTION IN ALL THE TENNIS STROKES, INCLUDING THE SERVE. EVEN THOUGH SOMETIMES A TENNIS PLAYER CAN USE A THROWING THOUGHT TO MAKE VARIOUS SHOTS, THAT DOES NOT MEAN HE SHOULD PRACTICE THAT. PRACTICING THE BEST WAY IS THE BEST PRACTICE. EVEN THOUGH ANY PRACTICE CAN MAKE YOU A LITTLE BETTER, YOU CAN ONLY REACH YOUR POTENTIAL WHEN YOU PRACTICE THE RIGHT STUFF. REMEMBER, THOUGH, ONLY RIGHT PRACTICE CAN MAKE YOUR SUCCESS FASTER AND MAKE YOU CLIMB HIGHER. TENNIS IS A HITTING ACTION. THE HITTING THOUGHT IS THE PRIMARY THOUGHT PATTERN. THE THROWING THOUGHT WILL MESS UP YOUR TRAINING FOR THE MECHANISM OF CONCENTRATION ON ALL LEVELS OF TENNIS PERFORMANCE.

NOW LET'S EMPHASIZE THE WORD "CONCENTRATION." THIS WORD, "CONCENTRATION," HAS BEEN USED SO OFTEN IT SEEMS IF YOU SAY "CONCENTRATION" PEOPLE WILL AUTOMATICALLY KNOW WHAT IT MEANS AND KNOW EXACTLY HOW TO CONCENTRATE. THIS IS TRUE IN THE GENERAL SENSE OF PAYING ATTENTION TO

CERTAIN THINGS ON CERTAIN OCCASIONS. IT IS FAR FROM THE TRUTH IN SPECIFIC SPORT PERFORMANCES.

IN A SPORT PERFORMANCE, THERE ARE SPECIFIC ATHLETIC ACTIONS. EVERY ACTION HAS ITS OWN SPECIFIC PARAMETERS. TO EXECUTE THOSE PARAMETERS PRECISELY IS THE ONLY WAY TO CONCENTRATE TO PERFORM THAT ACTION. IN MY MIND, CONCENTRATION IS TO KNOW EXACTLY HOW TO GET RID OF THE INTERFERENCE FACTORS. IF WE KNOW WHAT INTERFERES WITH WHAT WE DO, IT WILL BE EASIER TO CONCENTRATE. IF WE DO NOT KNOW WHAT INTERFERES AND HOW IT INTERFERES, HOW CAN WE CONCENTRATE?

INTERFERENCE FACTORS OF SPORT ACTIONS ARE MANY; SOME ARE MORE SERIOUS THAN OTHERS. IT DEPENDS ON WHAT YOU DO AND HOW IT INTERFERES WITH YOU. THERE ARE ACTION-ACTION INTERFERENCE, BALL INTERFERENCE, EYE INTERFERENCE, BIOMECHANICAL INTERFERENCE, PSYCHOLOGICAL INTERFERENCE, AND MOST IMPORTANTLY, INTELLECTUAL INTERFERENCE (BECAUSE YOU ARE TOO SMART IN ONE THING AND NOT SMART ENOUGH IN ANOTHER). WITHIN THIS GROUP OF INTERFERENCES, ONE IS MENTAL AND THE OTHER IS BIOMECHANICAL. THE MENTAL PART IS WHAT A PLAYER THINKS, SEES, FEELS, AND UNDERSTANDS. THE BIOMECHANICAL PART IS WHAT A PLAYER EXECUTES WITH HIS BODY. WE CAN ALSO CLASSIFY THE BIOMECHANICAL INTERFERENCE AS PREMENTAL INTERFERENCES. ONCE A PLAYER UNDERSTANDS WHAT HE SHOULD BE DOING, HE/SHE IS THINKING PROPERLY, AND THERE WILL BE NO INTERFERENCE. HE/SHE WILL BE ABLE TO CONCENTRATE PROPERLY. CONCENTRATION IS ON THE ACTION ITSELF, TO DO WHAT ONE SHOULD BE DOING WITHOUT SURRENDERING TO ANY OTHER THOUGHTS.

NOW LET ME GIVE YOU SOME EXAMPLES OF ACTION-ACTION INTERFERENCE: WHEN PLAYING FOOTBALL, A GOOD TIGHT END CATCHES THE BALL VERY WELL. IN A BIG MATCH, HE THINKS ABOUT RUNNING TOO EARLY AND HE MISSES A VERY IMPORTANT CATCH. IT IS THE RUNNING ACTION THAT INTERFERES WITH HIS CATCHING ACTION. A VERY HIGH-LIVES TENNIS PLAYER, HE GETS A SHORT SHOT FROM HIS OPPONENT. HE COULD EASILY FLIP HIS WRIST AND PUT THE POINT AWAY. HOWEVER, HE THINKS IT IS SO EASY TO PUT THE BALL IN A CERTAIN AREA ON THE OTHER SIDE OF THE COURT. HE TAKES HIS EYE AWAY FROM THE CONTACT, AND HE MISSES THE EASY PUT AWAY. (THE THROWING ACTION MESSED UP HIS HITTING ACTION.)

HERE, LET ME REPEAT THE GENERAL ATHLETIC PERFORMANCE LAWS:

1. FOR ANY SINGLE ATHLETIC ACTION, THERE IS A RESULT. THE RESULT IS AN INTERFERENCE FACTOR FOR THAT ACTION. THE CONCENTRATION OF THAT ACTION IS A FULL BIOMECHANICAL THOUGHT PATTERN OF THAT ACTION.

2. FOR ANY COMPOUND ATHLETIC ACTION—THAT IS, CATCH AND RUN, CATCH AND HIT, AND CATCH AND KICK—THE PRIMARY CONCENTRATION IS ALWAYS ON THE FIRST ACTION. THE SECOND ACTION IS THE INTERFERENCE FACTOR OF THE FIRST ACTION.

A FACTOR IS THE FEAR. WHAT HE NEEDS IS MENTAL TOUGHNESS. THAT MEANS HE DOES NOT CONSIDER ANYTHING ELSE; NO MATTER WHAT HAPPENS, HE JUST WANTS TO CATCH THE BALL. MENTAL TOUGHNESS CAN BE DEFINED AS "IF YOU KNOW WHAT IS RIGHT, THEN DO IT REGARDLESS."

NOW WE KNOW CATCHING AND RUNNING ARE CLEARLY TWO SEPARATE ACTIONS. EVEN TWO SEPARATE ACTIONS CAN CAUSE PLAYER PROBLEMS. IN TENNIS, A PLAYER TRIES TO DO A HITTING ACTION WITH A SWING MOTION, AND THIS SWING MOTION IS EXACTLY LIKE A THROWING ACTION. THE SEPARATION OF HITTING AND THROWING IS ONLY MENTAL. THEY ARE PRACTICALLY VERY SIMILAR. THESE TWO ACTIONS TAKE PLACE AT THE SAME TIME IN A UNIFIED FORM. THERE IS NO WAY WE CAN SEPARATE THEM BIOMECHANICALLY. THE ONLY WAY TO SEPARATE THEM IS TO THINK "I HIT" OR "I THROW." YOU CAN UNDERSTAND HOW DIFFICULT IS TO SEPARATE THE HIT AND THROW AT A SINGLE SWING. THEREFORE, ALL TENNIS STROKES SHOULD BE CALLED THE PRACTICE OF THE MECHANISM OF CONCENTRATION.

In tennis, it is using an action of hitting to make the contact. However, the player wants the ball to fly over the net and land on the other side of the court. The result is basically an action of throwing in nature. For us, whoever has used computer before, we can understand how we can use a certain program and want this program to do another different job. When we hit something, our eye looks here; the mind thinks "here." When we make a throw, our eyes tend to go there; the mind thinks "there." You can see how difficult it is under this confusion. This confusion will mess up the way we hit the ball. When we are hitting, we are making pure rotation. When we throw, we tend to extend during the releasing motion. The releasing motion tends to make tennis players hit the ball out long biomechanically. It can also cause the ball low to net the shot. If a player does not interfere with his shot, it is very difficult to correct these kind of mistakes. Usually it takes years for a player to go through self-learning and self-experience to find a certain way to play better. However, even the very best players still make these kinds of mistakes under pressure situations.

Playing the best tennis is to execute a complete system. This system contains several different actions. Each action is represented by a specific concentration. Here the word *action* and the word *concentration* are almost synonymous. A tennis player has to get to the ball first when running to the ball with a catching concentration. He then makes a swing to hit the ball with a hitting concentration. If he does not know what the hitting concentration is, then he will struggle with his game for years. Many players run and hit with great form and appear to be very talented; however, his game stay in his level can never overcome.

Hitting concentration is getting rid of the concept of throwing or minimizing the influence of the concept of throwing (placement) at the point of contact. Very few people understand why. Many coaches even teach the concept of throwing (placement) in tennis. Many talented athlete fall into the mental trap of a tennis game deeper and deeper, and they eventually give up the game. Many people struggle with their game, but they never give up. Their game will improve every time they have a chance to play, but they can never reach their potential in their tennis career.

I wish people who read my writing can think deeply about why I am writing about the sports concentration beginning with human hand structure. I wish the reader can understand the importance of human nature in general and that sports activities are part of our nature. What we think about profoundly influences the way we develop our ability to perform athletically. Let me repeat—what I am trying to emphasize is that as humans, we are too smart; we think too much. We think much more and more complex than required for the simple action of hitting. This is the reason I point out the importance of understanding the source of the intellectual interference.

Let me repeat again, when we swing our racket to hit a tennis ball, we use the action of hitting, doing the work like throwing. This job, in human minds, has a large component of the action of throwing in nature. Even though people understand what they are doing when they are hitting the ball, they still cannot concentrate to the degree of just hitting the ball. As I have stressed before, it is because the throwing concept is so strong in the mind of humans that players want to know the result right after the contact. It needs great discipline and a long time of practice to learn good concentration in a good hitting action. Usually concentration is not just either 100 percent or nothing. It can spread from 10 percent to 90 percent. It is difficult to get to 100 percent. How can we not think ahead at all when we are purposely performing the things we are hoping for? To think or to look where the object is going when we deliberately make this thing go where we want it to go is a natural thing. It is also an intelligent thing. Human are created to have this ability to think and to look ahead. This is the word *anticipation* in human language. When we do something, we anticipate a certain result. So anticipation is a part of the human intellectual system.

To think what humans think according to human intellectual ability may or may not be completely proper in sports performance. For example, the word *anticipation*, or the tendency to anticipate in playing tennis. If a player anticipates how fast the ball is coming and he/she runs fast to meet the ball, it is a good anticipation. If a player anticipates where the ball is going when he/she hits the ball, this is a bad anticipation. Just a slight idea of this anticipation for an incoming ball can help a player get where he wants to get. A slight anticipation of where the ball is going when he hits the ball can create an unforced error in a championship of a major tournament. A slight mental error can create tremendous problems biomechanically for a tennis player. To stop something in our mind that is what we normally think and normally do is a difficult thing. This is the reason we need thorough understanding of the game mentally and biomechanically with strict discipline and hard work to practice the mechanism of hitting concentration. I have stressed repeatedly on this point many times before. I hope the readers who are interested in tennis pay more attention to this point.

Concentration is action specific. In order to concentrate on a specific action, we have to have clear understanding of that action and clearly understand what interferes with that action in order to formulate proper concentration. If we do not know what the real interference factors are, how can we concentrate?

If you ask me, "You talk about concentration, concentration, concentration all the time—how about strategy?" my answer is, "For single play, the strategy is to make your opponent as uncomfortable, make it as difficult as possible. If you can get to every ball on your side of the court and hit the ball with good hitting concentration, you will be able to figure that out. For double play, you will be better off taking some lessons from experienced double player coaches."

No matter who is playing tennis, two things are the center of attention. The first is if you see a ball coming, how early and comfortable you can get there. The second is once a player gets to the ball, he/she has to make a good shot to finish he/her job. So to put it simply for any tennis player, these are the only two things you do.

So I would like to propose two simple athletic performance principles for athletic actions:

a. For every single athletic action, there is a result. The result is always the interference of that action.

    Explanation

    Actions are hitting, catching, throwing, kicking, blocking, pushing, etc.

b. For any compound athletic action (catch and run, hit and fly [golf], catch and throw, catch and kick), the primary concentration should always be on the first action; the second action is always the interference factor of the first action. The primary concentration should always be on the first action. The second action is a natural follow-up action. It is already programmed. You will do it automatically once the catch is made. If you need to catch and run and you just concentrate on the catch, you will never miss the run. If the action is catch and throw, you just concentrate on the catch and you will never miss the throw. If the compound action is catch and kick, you just concentrate on the catch and you will never miss the kick.

In tennis, two types of concentrations are essential. One concentration is to concentrate to get to the ball as early as possible. This is catching action concentration. If you ever think about how to hit the ball before you are ready to contact the ball, the hitting becomes an interference of your catching. The second one is concentrate to hit the ball. This is hitting action concentration. If you ever think about where you want to hit the ball, your hitting is already interfered with by the throwing action. In general, the hitting concentration is a natural transition. These catching and hitting programs are preplanned, and there is no other program that interferes in this operation. To get there and to hit smoothly depends on practice and the number of repetitions of these catching and hitting actions.

c.   Golf

Golf game is another product from the civilized world. I never swung a golf club until I was in my late seventies. I did not play golf when I was young because (1) it takes too much time to play and I could not get enough exercise and (2) it is much easier to find a tennis court and less expensive to play tennis than golf.

The game of golf must be coming from the game of hitting an object on the ground with a stick to begin with. If you hit an object on the ground with a stick, your swing has to be from upside down. From our human experience, there are very few cases we want to swing downward and expect the object to travel a long distance. There are very few occasions you want to hit something on the ground and wish this thing goes away as far as possible. To hit something away is often necessary, unless you are unable to throw it away with your hand. So the early game of golf must be developed much later in history than other hitting games, such as the early tennis like games.

The early game of golf was described in the book compiled by Sarah Baddie; it is how the *Mall Gazette* attempted to described the game in November 1868. The object is to drive a small gutta-percha ball in the smallest number of strokes into a succession of holes, scattering most of them at wide intervals from each other over some waste track of turf.

From what we can see how golf is developed today, we understand that human is capable of using human intelligence and imagination to create all kinds of games. Game play is part of human intellectual nature. There are physical games. There are intellectual games. Sports activities are basically physical games. What we are interested in are the physical actions involved in those games.

Golf is using an action of hitting to perform a job like throwing. The purpose is to make a little white ball travel a certain distance in a specific direction into a little hole. The reasons we can play golf are all because humans invented the golf clubs. Now let's us give a hypothetical example. Assuming there is no golf club that ever existed in the world, and there were a game like the present golf game today. People have to throw the little white ball in different distances and toss and row and finally put the little white ball into that little hole. We can call this a "throwing golf." People practice their technique in throwing rather than hitting. Actually, it is not too bad to have a game like that. Better yet, if people can make the total time required to finish the game as a factor in final score and people have to run through the nine holes, it would be a very demanding game to play.

Fortunately, people invented the golf club. The golf club is designed with specific directional and distance control to replace the throwing action.

After people invented the golf club, the golf swing becomes a typical action of hitting. This hitting is similar to the hitting actions in baseball and tennis except the ball is on the ground. Just because the ball is on the ground, so people have to design the golf clubs as what the clubs are today. The golf club with its shape and different angles are designed to do this specific job—that is to hit a ball on the ground and let the ball fly a certain distance.

What I am trying to emphasize here is that the physical actions of hitting and throwing are part of our human nature. Once we change the nature of the action, we naturally change the way we think. Now we change from a game of "throwing golf" to a game of "hitting golf." Of course, there are certain strokes in the game of golf. Some stroke still like a throwing action, such as short games in a pitching stroke or a putting stroke. Tee-off strokes will be complete hitting strokes.

How can I get a balanced golf swing? As we discussed previously many, many times, a good hitting action is a localized action. It is a pure rotational motion. It simply means "here I swing." The best way to feel it is to make a swing at a pretended object on the ground and do an empty swing. The proper mental thought is, *I just want to hit this staff here*. With this swing thought, your back swing and forward swing will be more pure rotational and it will not cause you any balance problem. A balanced swing is absolutely necessary for your golf game. Here, I have to point out that the golf ball is an interference factor for your golf swing in terms of your balance, because once the contact is made, the ball flies out. If you have any thought of letting your swing follow the ball, it will cause you a serious balance problem. Also, there should not be any distance consideration during a golf swing. The distance is determined by which club you are using. That means when you make a golf swing, you do not adjust your swing to decide the distance. Instead, you use a different club with same type of swing to decide the distance you are making. Of course, putting the ball is a different action. The putting action is like pushing or a gentle throwing action.

How can I get max distance? There are three factors that determine your max distance: (1) your club head of the back swing has to be at your max backward position, (2) the initial velocity of your down swing has to be as fast as you can, (3) your body weight has to be behind the contact point, and (4) your eyesight has to be kept at the position of contact until you have completed your swing. The final acceleration of your wrist is the most important part of the whole golf swing process.

With the various factors in mind, of course, the proper biomechanical swing has to be there. This proper swing is your consistent swing. This is the most important part of your golf game. You have your own physical limitation. You may not be able to swing as fast as other people. You may not be as flexible as other people. Proper use of your body is the most critical factor. The critical joints are the knee, the shoulder, and the wrist. The less use of your elbow, the better.

The hitting action of tennis and the hitting action of golf are similar except tennis requires precise eye-hand coordination mechanism; golf does not require precise eye-hand coordination mechanism. When you play tennis, you see a ball coming. When your eye estimates the distance your hand can reach the ball, then you make the swing. Your eyes estimate the distance for your hand to react, then your hand acts. This is what we usually call the eye-hand coordination process. This is a dynamic situation. If you close your eyes, you can never play the game of tennis.

It is different in golf. The golf swing is a static swing. The golf ball on the ground does not move. If any person can address the ball properly, he does not have to see the ball to hit the ball. This is the reason a blind person can play golf and there are blind golfers that hit a hole in one at times. A blind person can never play tennis.

For any golfer, the most important thing is to find his/her own consistent swing motion without considering the distance of the ball's flight.

The most important mental problem for golfers, in my mind, is the interference of the little white ball with the eyes of the golfers when he/she makes the swing. It is because the eyes see the ball; once the eyes see the ball, the mind loses the sense of the swing, especially for average golfers. It takes years for someone to establish a consistent swing, and then you can see the ball and also know what you want to do to the ball. At the same time, you still consciously know and feel your swing. So the mental problem for golfers is how you can ignore the moving ball and concentrate to establish a consistent swing of your own. Then use a different club to establish your hitting distance with the same swing. The real devil is, the ball moves after the contact, and the golfer wants to control the ball before he/she has established his/her consistent golf swing.

The most detrimental factor to influence concentration of golf swing is the little white ball. If you practice your swing aiming at a piece of grass, you will find your swing almost perfect every time. If you put a little white ball there to hit, everything breaks down. How can we concentrate then? Concentration is putting your mind on the action you are doing. Think about the body movement and ignore the ball. The important parameters of your swing are the shoulder, the knee, and the wrist. The location and movement of these parameters have to be consistent in your swing.

d. Soccer

A human is a dual mutual complementary system. The human brain has a right half and a left half. The human body has an upper half and a lower half. The human body has a right half and a left half. Both halves are never meant to be exactly the same; they, however, complement each other and become a common living body. This is, in essence, the human system. This is the best survival system.

We have talked so far about the upper-extremity sports. We know that the two athletic systems of human body are equally important. The upper-extremity sports system and the lower-extremity sports system are actually one in what we call the human athletic system. One system does not work without the other in terms of human action and survival. The human athletic system is exactly like the human itself. The marriage of a male and a female creates life. The marriage of the upper- and lower-extremity sports saves lives. Without combination of the two athletic systems, a human is just a piece of meat. Without the combination of these two athletic systems, there will be absolutely no word as *survival* in the human vocabulary.

It is apparent that the lower biolink system was much more important for the survival of human race historically to begin with. Running away from danger was the rule of thumb for survival in the old civilization.

The human hand is the most important hardware in the human system. The human power hand grip is responsible for human survival. The human hand precision grip was responsible for the development of tools and civilization. The upper biolink system and the lower biolink system string together seamlessly as the human kinetic system and are responsible for the survival and development of the human race. Both hands and feet are the reason humans and the world are the way they are today. The lower biolink system is inclined toward physical development, and the upper biolink system is inclined toward the mental development. The lower athletic system is from the hip joint down to the toes. It is a left-right-left-right rotational system with the sacrum in the middle. It is very similar to the upper athletic system. The shoulder joint corresponds to the hip joint. The elbow joint corresponds to the knee joint, and the wrist joint corresponds to the ankle joint. The lower athletic system performs the running, jumping, and kicking athletic actions. Here, in a soccer game, we concentrate on the kicking action and the ball controlled by the feet.

Catching Action

The first action in soccer is also a catching action. In soccer, catch is not catching with the hand. It is catching with the feet. As we mentioned before, in the upper-extremity sports, the catching action is very aggressive mentally. In order to catch, you have to get there first. The physical part of the catching action is the ability to run. The mental part of the catching action is how to think and use your eyes properly to make an early start to run to the ball.

This catching action is similar to the catching action of the upper-extremity sports, except this is using the foot to kick rather than using the implement to hit. The only thing different is that you may have to fight off other people who may also try the same thing as you do. At the time, when you are trying so hard to get to the ball, you have to keep your eyes wide open. To make a pass right away should be your first choice. To catch the ball and bring it up front is only the second choice. The ball travels much faster than the human can run. More passes in soccer during the games is the best strategy. What happens if you don't have a teammate to pass to? Then you have to control the ball. Running, catching, and controlling the ball are the most important skills for any soccer player. Just as basketball players have to practice rebounds and dribbles, soccer players have to develop the running and good footwork to be an outstanding soccer player.

There is no secret for developing any good foot skill. It is just the more you do, the better you get. Here, we have to use an old Chinese philosophy: "Fancy skills come from repetition of basic skills." If you watch how the professional basketball players dribble the ball today, you will understand what I mean. I also want to remind people that it is much easier to build foot skills from the player as young and as early as possible.

Kicking Action

The kicking action is the most powerful action in the human athletic system because of the anatomical and the skeletal and muscular structure of the lower extremities. The kicking action was the most useful in close body combat in the primitive historical times. The invention of the game soccer was also parallel to the invention of the upper-extremity games historically. Sports, games, music, and arts are all timely products that emerged from the evolution of the civilization. The action of kicking itself is not a team sport; it is just an independent single human physical movement. It is a protective physical action for human survival. It is also an innate action. It is ingrained in the human neurological system. Humans are born to kick and even learn to kick before they are born. You can ask any mother during late pregnancy. Like any other survival actions, it gradually develops into a sport.

The kicking action has its own physical and mental parameters. The physical parameters of kicking are simple, and they are just biomechanical in nature. The mental parameters are similar to that of the upper extremity (the hands).

There are two areas of the kicking skill a soccer player is absolutely essential. One area is the ball control. Just like we have mentioned in a previous paragraph, this skill requires years of practice with a passion of just loving to control the ball with the feet. It includes many fake movements to keep the ball away from your opponent. Keep in mind that it is real skill to control the ball, not just fancy movements; otherwise you will lose the ball.

Since soccer is a team sport, passing first is always a good strategy. Always keep your eyes wide open. To pass the ball to one of your open teammates is the best quality of a soccer player. The ball travels much faster than the players run. Better soccer teams always have more passes in their games. Passing requires precision. Now we can see that passing is using a kicking action to do a job as throwing action. When you make a throwing action, either with your hand or your feet, the relation of the eyes and either your hand or feet is always the same. Here, this is an identical situation as in tennis. In tennis, it is the concept of hitting and throwing. In soccer, it is the concept of kicking and throwing.

Passing in soccer requires both physical and mental concentration. Passing is a simple kicking action. It requires the player to have an open, relaxed vision to see exactly where he is trying to pass before the contact is made; also his eyes have to concentrate at the contact point (on the ball) until he finishes his kicking action. The thing to remember here is, if you try to see where the ball is going before you finish your kicking action, you will compromise your kicking action.

There is another interference biomechanically. We all know that the kicking action is from the hip down to the toes; the hip joint is the main source of power. When a player wants to make a strong kick, he tends to kick his foot up and, at the same time, tilts his upper trunk backward. In his mind, while tilting his upper trunk backward, it may be relatively easier to raise the other leg up in his kick action; however, it is just the opposite. The tilt of the upper body, in reality, slows down the rotation of the hip, which is the source of power for the kicking action. It is a mental trap for people to learn the kicking action to begin with. This problem comes from the interference from the ball. The golden rule is, whatever sports action we do, our thought should always be on the action itself.

e. Ski

Ski motion is when you wear a pair of very long shoes walking or running down a very slippery slope. Of course, no matter what the surface is, you must learn to walk before you can run. If you want to participate in a running race, that is another level of what you want to do. First, let's talk about walking down the slippery slope.

There are two things we have to prevent if we want to have any enjoyment on the snow slope: the first is we have to avoid the skis crossing each other, and second is we have to know how to stop.

In order to prevent the skis crossing each other, we either have to walk just straight ahead or we have to move both feet almost at the same time during the step alteration to avoid both feet crossing each other. There are a few things very mental in skiing, just like in all other sports.

Skiing is a lower-extremity sport. Any movement in directional change requires step alternation. Alternating steps forward is the definition of forward movement. A forward movement is a balance-unbalance-balance process. It is a natural weight shifting process. If the movement is not on the snow, racing in skis is another story. Under the slippery condition, downhill racing can reach very high velocity. Total body control and balance control is critical. Let the lower body take control completely. Usually, any extra effort comes in first from the upper body. It is wise to not make too much extra effort when you are running smoothly.

1. A human is a dual mutual complimentary common living body. Skiing is the job of the lower athletic system. The upper athletic system plays the role of just helping the lower athletic system. When we ski, our concentration should always be on the lower body. The upper body should be totally relaxed and follow the lower body.
2. Weight shifting is an action of balancing. Don't be afraid of shifting your weight.
3. Weight shifting is the mechanism of direction changing.
4. The direction changing is always on the leading (front) ski.
5. When you try to turn right with your lower body, your eye should look to the left and vice versa.
6. The off-weight ski always follows the direction of the ski with the body weight.
7. The weight is always on the down-slope ski.

All the above points are basic principles to learn when skiing. These are the fundamental concepts of walking down a slippery slope with extra-long shoes. In case of a ski race, it will be similar to running down the slippery slope. In the ski race, the important thing is the close unification of the upper athletic system and the lower athletic system. Keep the upper body tightly close to the lower body; minimize the feeling of extension of the upper body. See everything along the way to the location you want to go, but do not focus on any object specifically.

Last but not least, I want to make a suggestion for everyone who likes to ski or teaches skiing: the best way, I think, to teach is to start by teaching the stop. Teach that the hockey stop is better than the snow plow. The reasons are simple:

1. Learning to stop will get rid of the feeling of fear. On the slope, the most scary thing is not knowing how to stop when you are in trouble.
2. On the slope, weight shifting is not natural because of the slipperiness. Learn a hockey stop with the left foot, and the right foot at downslope alternatively will have already completed a full turn. This is the best or most efficient way to learn to turn when we ski.

23

Mechanism of Concentration of Hitting Action

A. Attention and Focus

The two words *attention* and *focus* have been used so often it seems there is no need to explain at all. Once you say them, everybody will automatically understand what it means and what they should do. This is true in many, many cases. It is also not applicable in many, many cases. I feel there is need to explain further about these two words in order to formulate the proper mechanism of concentration.

The word *attention* has been explained as an act or faculty of mentally concentrating on a single object, thought, or event, especially in preference to other stimuli. The word *focus* has been described as a central point, as of attraction, attention, or activity. If we consider the meaning of the three words—attention, focus, and concentration—literally, there seems to be very little difference among them. I prefer to use the word *concentration* because the word *attention* is too general. It represents a general mental state of performance. Attention is too broad in my mind. There is also a mechanism of division of attention. So we usually say we can concentrate on our attention; however, we usually do not say the opposite. The word *focus* does not have the weight mentally as the word *concentration* in athletic performance; therefore, I prefer to use the word *concentration*.

B. Concentration

I want to say this first: concentration is action specific in sport performance. I am going to say this again and again and again. Concentration on hitting is a mental process. It involves, generally, how a person prepares himself/herself mentally and physically to start and finish an action described as a hitting action. This hitting action has different connotations at different occasions at different times, such as hitting in baseball, hitting in tennis, hitting in golf, hitting in hockey, hitting in ping-pong, hitting in racket ball, and hitting in hand ball. The rules may be different, the purpose may be different, the swing strength may be different, and the direction of swing may be different. They, however, have a common mental process to carry out these different biomechanical movements. Here, we are interested in the mental process because this is the most important portion of the action and is often misunderstood by players and coaches.

The mental process begins with what you are thinking on your mind. What you think determines what you do. So first you have to know—not just know, you have to understand—and clearly and strongly believe you know exactly what you are going to do. This is the beginning of the concentration process. We can call this the state of mental toughness. It is a state of mind of strong determination and a fearless mentality to do exactly what you know you should be doing. You do not consider the result. You let your action tell the result. It sounds very complicated, but it is not. For example, in tennis, this mental process could just be just wanting to get there. This is executing a catching concentration. Or "I just want to swing through completely without any hesitation"—this is executing the hitting concentration.

The first step of concentration is to filter out some irrelevant thoughts or noncritical thoughts and some peripheral thoughts. Your center thought should be a single simple thought. The most common athletic thoughts are catch, hit, throw, block, spin, jump, run, etc. If any thought is not an action itself directly, it is a peripheral thought. If any thought is the result of an action, it is a peripheral thought.

In tennis, the first thought is to get there. To prepare to get there is to bounce your two feet and be ready to take off. Keep your eyes wide open and look in the direction where the ball may come from. You should feel a strong movement of your hip and your knee joint. Even though this is your footwork, do not think about your feet. Think that your feet will slow you down. Your footwork starts from your hip joint and not your feet. When I say you feel, I mean you just feel. It is an awareness feeling. If you feel too strongly, it will become your thought. That strong feel will interfere with your vision. Take a return serve in tennis as an example. You must see the ball, the toss, the server's movement, and the sound of the server's contact with the ball as the overall cues to anticipate the coming ball. Here, the word *anticipation* is very important. You use the word see for everything, but the concentration is on the ball. Do not try to focus your eyes on the ball too hard. You must be intense physically and relaxed mentally. There should be no strain mentally to use all your sensory imputes to handle the coming ball. If you are too tense mentally and overuse your eyes to see too hard or to think something other than just meet the ball, the ball will pass by you. It is very important not to think of hitting the ball until you are ready to contact the ball. For example, if you try to see at the coming ball too hard, you will definitely be late to meet the ball. Most importantly—I want to repeat—do not think of anything else except just meeting the ball. You must relax your vision to see a fast-moving object. Your eyes have a retention time. If you see the moving object too hard, you are always going to be later than the moving object.

The previous paragraph is the concentration to get to the ball. The purpose of getting to the ball is to make a hit. You do not have to think about hit when you first start to run to the ball, but as you run closer to the ball, you will automatically think about hitting the ball. The preaction of hitting is the back swing of your racket. It is to prepare you to make your hit. This is the reason I think there are certain things the coach does not have to teach. For example, a great number of coaches still ask their students to get the racket back. What I am trying to say is that "Get the racket back" is automatic, and this thought is very strong in a player's mind to begin with. We even ask the player not to think about this before he/she starts running to the ball. How could he/she forget to swing his/her racket after he/she gets there? You do not have to teach it, especially to emphasize it, because if the student is faithfully thinking of getting the racket back, most likely he will miss his shot. It is true that most players do not have a full swing. If you want to teach a player to make the absolute full swing, you can teach the student to practice the full swing every time they play and make the full swing a habit whenever they play and whenever the swing time is allowable. It is true that in the hitting motion, the bigger the range of your back swing, the greater will be your impact force of your forward swing at contact. Try to build a specific hitting habit in general practice sessions. In the process of hitting, the important thing to emphasize is the concept of "here." It is proper to stress the concept of spinning in the hitting process. The spin concept is also a localized action, "here." It is also important even not to think about hitting at all before you are ready to make the contact. You will know exactly where to hit the ball once you are ready to make the contact. I want to repeat it: when you are trying to get to the ball, nothing else should be on your mind, except "get to the ball." All these happen in a matter of just a few seconds in today's tennis matches. Do not worry—you are not going to miss your hit if you can get to the ball. I want to repeat it: you will not miss your swing. The swing is automatic once you get there. The type of swing and your comfort with the swing is the thing you need to practice. Now you're ready to make a hit.

Hitting in tennis is only a matter of a split second. It is from the swing forward until the swing is finished.

The mental part of hitting is as follows: Your mind is at the point of contact. Your thought about your swing is at the point of contact. Your eyes look at the location of contact, even though you cannot see much, maybe just a blur of ball and racket movement. Keeping your mental elements at the location of contact is the essence of the hitting concentration.

It is difficult to see the contact clearly; however, it is important that your eyes have to be at the location of the point of contact. Where is the contact point then? It is on the ball. It is on the lower part of the ball, and it is directly behind the ball in the direction where you want the ball to go on your hitting. When I say it is at the lower part of the ball, it is very important. How low depends on your general practice when you practice your game. After your swing, there is no ball. The ball is on its way to the destination you want the ball to go. You should still feel your swing in the process of finishing up (this is what I call the after-hitting feeling). Let me repeat this: this is what I call the after-hitting feeling. The sense of completion of your swing is very critical. Only when you have this feeling do you complete your swing. This is the only way you are able to make precision shots. To finish the hitting or complete the hitting is very, very critical in the game of tennis. I am going to repeat, repeat, and repeat this point: this is the hitting concentration.

The most detrimental interference for this concentration of hitting is mental. It is the fact that at the time when the contact is made, the ball flies to a certain target area. That means at the contact point, a throwing action also takes place. We have talked about this again and again. Since hitting and throwing are the innate survival actions of humans, it is a part of the neurological system and wired in the human brain. It is very difficult to separate the results of these two actions clearly at the point of contact at the same time. If you close your eyes when you make the swing, your feeling is only your swing and you feel you just made a hit. If you had your eyes open and you can see the ball, it is difficult to not track the ball and to see where it is going. I have mentioned this before. I said, "The eye is the leader dog of the blind." I have also mentioned that the eyes open up with only one goal and one purpose: it is to collect information and give all the information to the brain for the brain to plan and react. When you have your eyes open, you see your opponent, you see the net, and you see where there is an open area. When you are making a swing, how can you avoid not having the feeling of where you are eager for the ball to go? This is our human intelligence. However, this becomes our distraction when we play tennis. This is the reason I am writing this book. We can say that it is our eyes that complicate the way we play the game. It is true. Can we correct this interference? Yes, we can, if we can play with the concentration as I have just described in the previous section.

For the purpose of survival, our eyes have to be active. All the information collected from our eyes is the life we live. Our eyes work so hard God creates the night for our eyes to rest. Once we get up in the morning, the eyes start to work. It collects all the information for the brain (mind) to plan for the day.

The mind is the master. However, without the help of the eyes, the mind is just like a black box. The brain stores all the information collected by the eyes from the past and to the present and stores them in the memory bank. It helps to plan for the future. All the information is gradually translated into projects and actions. This is the way the human system works.

Helping your children is a natural thing. When my children started hitting the ball, my mind started thinking about the game. I tried to hit the ball against the wall. I also tried to hit the ball with my wife. Of course, you can imagine how two people who had never played tennis before looked like playing tennis. I did not want to take lessons. I did not want to read tennis books. I always want to learn things from my own experience.

Even if you do not want to take lessons, you cannot avoid listening to many different lessons. I remember there were so many times people gave lessons to students next to the court we were playing; there were so many times people gave lessons to their partners whom they were playing with. Anyhow, the lessons I heard were many. However, the best lesson I heard was from a young boy. He was about six or seven years old. He was playing and teaching another boy about the same age, and he was playing with another boy about his age. I am just guessing their ages. But the two really looked very similar in age. Within about forty minutes, that little boy coach said just one sentence: "Swing from low to high!" He was the only one who said the least among all the people trying to teach other people on the court.

Sometimes when I hear a coach say something making some sense, I stop and watch and listen to what else he says and what else I can learn. Now it reminds me of a story. More than twenty years ago, I was on my way to the East Coast, passing by Silver Spring, Maryland. I stopped at a tennis club to see their tennis activities. I saw one coach was giving a lesson to an aged lady. I heard a statement: "Do not control the ball, just control your own swing. That is the only thing you can control." I was impressed with that statement. So I stopped there and asked him if we could talk for a few minutes after his lesson. He said yes.

We had a meeting after his lesson, and we talked about tennis teaching and our thoughts about the game. His name was Jeff Klein, and he was the tennis director of a private tennis club at Silver Spring, Maryland. We became good friends. We have learned from each other in the game of tennis since that brief meeting twenty years ago. A tennis game is a microcosm of the process of life. To learn the game of tennis at any time at any occasion is good for anybody who is interested in the life process. Success in the game and success in personal life requires the same personal ingredients.

To be successful in tennis, one must follow certain basic principles: (1) have a strong desire to be successful—that means work hard; (2) always do the first thing first; (3) take every action faithfully and thoroughly; (4) concentrate on all actions; and (5) know when to be intense and when to be relaxed.

Different people learn things differently. It is absolutely individual dependent. It does not matter how a person learns; the important thing is people must learn. Unfortunately, many tennis players, after they reach a certain level, lose their impetus for learning.

Whenever I am on the court, I try everything to challenge my own judgment. For every mental parameter, I usually repeat-test it at least more than a hundred times before I can validate my own feeling.

Just wanting to learn the game from scratch is like jumping into the ocean to learn how to swim without any previous swimming experience. Even though I did not take lessons and did not read books, it does not mean I did not want to acquire the real knowledge about the game. Actually, I was so hungry and eager to know the real truth of the game since my children were interested in the game, and nothing is more important to me than knowing which is a really good book to read and what person is telling the real truth. You can imagine how desperate I was and how helpless I felt. I was in complete darkness and desperate to see some light.

The difficulty was very much related to my own personality and my own habit of learning in my life. When I learn something, I cannot go forward if there is anything I do not understand. I feel uncomfortable when I skip something. That is the reason I am a slow reader. It was the same way I learned the game of tennis. I wanted to know where the game was coming from, and I also wanted to know where it was going. I wanted to think through everything myself rather than to read what other people said. Of course, this is the way I learn about sports, not the way I learn about mathematics, chemistry, or physics. I think I did mention a story previously. When I saw my granddaughter was tossing small pieces of stone underhanded, she changed into a full overhanded throwing motion when I asked her to throw the stone farther. Children take command of doing the things they know they can do. This is the reason I want to see children play the game. I decided to sit by the court side in one of the tennis clubs in Ann Arbor to watch when the children take lessons. One thing I know is that children play the game according to what they know, and they play according to their own physiology. The purpose of my doing so was twofold: (1) I wanted to see and hear how the tennis pros teach, and (2) I wanted to know how the children would interpret the instruction and react with their own minds. Certainly, concentration was one of the factors too.

It was so clearly demonstrated that almost all the children have a very strong feeling of throwing in their system. They turn their head to see where the ball is going every time they contact the ball. This makes the concentration of hitting so difficult to learn, especially when the hitting action creates a throwing result. I have mentioned this many, many times before; l have to mention it again. I think the more you read it, the better and deeper understanding you will have.

Here, we have to mention about the concept of anticipation. The concept of anticipation is in our system whether we want it or not. Sometimes it is good for us, and sometimes it is bad for us, as far as the athletic actions are concerned. For example, if we anticipate the ball is coming in a catching action, it is good. If we anticipate where the ball is going in a hitting action, the anticipation is bad. However, it is a part of our mental attitude; we can control it. The ability to anticipate is a part of human intellectual ability. When we do something, we do anticipate a certain result. Under normal situations, there is nothing wrong if we can finish the word do properly. When we do things properly, the result will be just like we anticipated.

We must understand that the word do is the action involved. In a hitting action, the word do is simply the swing. The concentration should be on the word do only. The concentration has two separate parts. The concentration of the word do has a mental part and a biomechanical part. The mental part is what is on the player's mind, how the player feels, and how and what the player sees or focuses on when the player makes the swing. The physical part or the biomechanical part of the concentration is how that player's swing looks like physically when we take a picture with a camera.

Suppose today is a good day and I decide to sit by the court side to watch the children to play. I often see little kids made so many unforced errors and are so frustrated. They yell at themselves, "Stupid, Grandmother can do it." They do know that they did not use their eyes properly. They do not how what the relation of anticipation with the action is. They do not know how to concentrate mentally. They do not know what a complete swing is. They just play according to their own intelligence. This is why I call all the interference intellectual interference.

We also know that if we let our mind take over, that means we think properly with our mind. Everything will be OK.

Now we know the mind is the master. Our mind is the only organ that can control our eyes. All we have to do is to tell the eyes, "Don't look" or "close up"; the trouble is that our eye is also part of our mind. Even when our eyes are closed, our mind may still think about what we should not be thinking. This is the reason it is so difficult to get rid of some of the mental interferences. This is the reason it is so difficult for a golfer to think about his swing when he sees the little white ball he is trying to hit. However, we know the mind is still the master. If the mind initiates something else to think about, this different thought is what we used to say: "We change our mind." This new thought will block the early thought and the eye function. With this in mind, for example, if we think to spin the ball at the point of contact, our eyes will not track where the ball is going. There are so many cues we can use at the moment the racket meets the ball such as to say the following: "action," "hand," "finish," "hard," or "through." The main idea is to think of something and let the thought process prevent the eye from tracking the ball. As we stated before, if you do not think and say the word *hit*, you will feel like you just made a hitting action, but your eyes move before you finish your action and this is a mixed hitting and throwing action. Because hitting and throwing are so strong in the human mind, this becomes a part of human nature. Let me stress this again—this is part of human nature, and humans are born with this inclination. This was expressed by how human hands are structured. Human psychology follows the human anatomical structure. When you make the swing with your arm and hand, it is difficult not to think where you want the ball to go. It is difficult for you not to see where you would like the ball to go. This conflict becomes the mental trap for tennis players playing the game and for golfers to play golf, especially for beginners and amateur players. It took many, many years for professional players to play the way they are playing. Even at the highest level of competition, under pressure, many unforced errors could also happen because of this interference.

There are many clichés in tennis coaching such as "Keep your eyes on the ball," "Hit the ball," "Don't worry where the ball is going," "Racket back," "Follow throw," and "Keep your head down." These are all the efforts by coaches to help players to overcome these kinds of interferences.

> Many years ago, I proposed a word to define what the game of tennis should be. This word is catchithrow. That means when we play tennis, we are doing three athletic actions: catch, hit, and throw. It is coincidental that the last letter of the word catch is *h* and this *h* is the first letter of the word hit; the last letter of the word *hit* is *t*, and this *t* is the first letter of the word throw. Therefore, tennis is a game of catch, hit, throw. If we want to play the game well, we have to get there first— that is the action catch; this catch is like any catch in any sport we have today. After we get there, it becomes

a hit naturally. Once the hit action takes place, the ball is gone. We have to forget about the action of throwing now. However, our eyes (and our mind) really want to know where the ball is going and where the ball lands; that is the result of the throwing action. Therefore, after we make the swing to hit the ball, we cannot help but still think where we want the ball to go, and we still watch and hope where we want the ball to land. Now you can see how the game makes people think. If we do not analyze the game, students will not understand what is wrong when something happens to them. The mental parts are as follows: the first thing is, the player has to get there. The hitting action requires the eyes at contact point; we have to forget about the throwing action. If we want to play tennis well, the action of catching and the word *catch* is the most important word. At the end of the catch, it becomes the word *hit*. Once you finish the hit just think you've finished your throw already because the hit and throw are identical biomechanically. Do not let the throwing thought linger to damage a perfect hitting action.

In the game of tennis, the concept of throwing becomes the most detrimental mental problem of the game itself. Throwing is related to the concept of distance. Throw and change the location to "there" from "here." When you throw, make your arm extend rather than pull it back in. These concepts confuse the eye mentally and affect the body biomechanically.

The most detrimental mental problem in a game millions of people play and that thousands of coaches coach in the modern world has never been thoroughly investigated and exposed. Thousands of young people suffer and are frustrated when they start to learn the game of tennis. If you teach a young child the difference between hitting and throwing, they clearly understand the difference because hitting and throwing are part of their neurological system. If you ask them to hit the ball to somewhere and let them not pay any attention to where the ball is going, that is difficult. This is the reason so many kids get very frustrated when they make unforced errors. They do not know all they need is a good hit. A good hit will send the ball to where it is suppose to be going. The natural direct way is, of course, to think where the ball is going when they hit the ball. They do not know that their way of thinking interferes with what they are doing. Making the matter worse is that many coaches use the concept of throwing to teach the action of hitting. This way enhances the misconception of the student. It is true that they may get better with their game just doing it the way they do. However, it will certainly prevent them from developing into the highest level of tennis player. Let me repeat this: both the hitting and throwing are parts of our neurological system, and the throwing concept is the strongest. We have to use the proper hitting cue to block out the throwing concept, then tennis will become the most enjoyable game a human has ever played.

It is unfortunate that when somebody learns tennis, it is very easy for a coach to make a soft throwing motion and guide the ball to the other side of the court. Coaches usually ask their student to do as they do. The players automatically think that is the right way of playing the game. Many coaches will say, "I do not care what they think. As long as they enjoy the game and get some exercise, that will be fine." I totally agree with them. I know there is a difference between coaching a serious tennis player and teaching somebody with limited physical ability just to get some exercise. However, I think it is still better to provide students with proper concept, no matter what their physical ability and purpose is.

I call all the mistakes and the unforced errors caused by the mixed-up feeling of the two survival actions of hitting and throwing intellectual interferences because to see where the ball is going and to think where the ball is going to be land are human intelligence. They do what humans usually should be doing. However, playing tennis should not be that way because the action we are doing is actually a hitting action. The result of that action is exactly like we are throwing the ball. It is very hard for us not to have the feeling of just throwing the ball. But if we have that feeling, it will prevent us to become the best tennis players we can be. Many teenagers fall into that trap for years before becoming a better tennis player. I have seen many frustrated teenagers smash rackets on the ground, yelling loudly after they make a mistake and yell at themselves, "Stupid, Grandma can do it." They cannot believe how they missed such an easy shot. They do not realize that they turn their head when they hit the ball and their eyes move away when they contact the ball and they want the ball to go where they want it to go. These mental conditions create biomechanical errors. They do not know they extended their arm at contact rather than pull their arm back around their body. They even think about how to hit the ball before they get to the ball. They think about where the ball us going rather than think about their stroke. They think this way because they are human and they are smart. That is human intelligence. How can they not be frustrated when the unforced error happened?

Coaches usually will tell their students to concentrate. The students usually thought they are already in good concentration. You can see how frustrated the players could be.

I collected more than a dozen broken and twisted tennis rackets just to remind me how much these kids are frustrated. I did not have broken rackets from my own children, may be they knew they could not afford to have another racket. However, I did see on many different occasions their frustrated manners.

All these are part of the reason that attracts me into the game of tennis. I cannot get out of it and have the peace of mind to live until I really know why so many things should not be happening and happen in such a beautiful game.

Where the Frustration of a Tennis Player comes from

Once you get into the game, you like to play the game. You feel comfortable after you have played. We all need the exercise, and it is our nature of doing our own things. It comes from our survival instinct. Tennis players usually like to practice. They are willing to do whatever needed to improve their mental and physically skills. As coaches, tennis parents, and tennis researchers, our goal is to minimize students' frustration and make them learn the easiest way and progress the fastest way to accomplish what they can accomplish. So we have to know three things: (1) where their frustration comes from, (2) what causes their frustration, and (3) how we can solve their problems.

1. The important thing for any tennis player is to get to the ball first and then to make a good hit. If a tennis player fails to get to the ball and misses a shot, he/she usually understands why, because he either waits for the ball to bounce or does not aggressively run to the ball. Even though he made a mistake, but he knows why. He/she will not be unreasonably frustrated, because he knows that getting there or not is a very simple thing and he/she can correct that. Of course, sometimes it is just impossible for him/her to get there. There is not much he/she can do when these things happen. He knows better than anyone else what is wrong. He will try to correct the situation and not let the same mistake happen again. Sometimes he does need the coach's reminder.

    During the catching phase, if a player does not get to the ball, the mistake is usually mental. If the player has been properly instructed about the mental concentration of catching, the player should clearly understand the consequence of what caused that mistake. Knowing the reason will not cause frustration.

2. The player gets to the ball comfortably and makes a swing. In the player's mind, it should be a very easy shot to make, but it was an unforced error. The ball was out of bounds or the ball stopped on his own side of the net.

Here, it is a typical hitting mistake. Without going any further, we know the player will make an immediate reaction. If he knows exactly what was wrong and knows how to correct that mistake, he will not react violently to that kind of mistake because that kind of mistake has happened many times before and he knows how to correct them. The bottom line is whether he had been instructed with the detailed mechanism of concentration as we previously discussed. As a matter of fact, if the player was instructed properly and he/she practices his/her hitting concentration when these things happen, he/she will just smile and think, *I will not let this simple mistake happen again*, and he/she will not be frustrated. Usually, frustration comes from the player knowing what really happened.

It is extremely important for a tennis player to know that whenever he/she makes a mistake on the court, he/she should be the one to know exactly what happened and why. If he/she feels he/she does not know, he/she should ask his/her coach and tell the coach why. It is equally important that if he/she feels his/her mistake is not like his/her coach mentioned, he/she must point out what he/she thinks caused that mistake. Discussion is the best way to solve these kind of problems.

It is also extremely important for coaches to understand that it is their responsibility to diagnose the student's mistake precisely and let the students know exactly what mistake happened and give the student proper instruction. The coach should point out precisely, either mentally or biomechanically, how to correct that mistake. The coach's goal is to let the students know exactly why the mistake occurs precisely; it is either mental or biomechanical. So the students can diagnose and correct their own mistakes independently on the court in the future.

Concentration is both mental and biomechanical. This is the nature of the game in athletics. You need to make your decision mentally. You need to execute the physical action biomechanically. The physical and mental aspects of what you do are just like two sides of the same coin. You do the things you know. What you know is mental, and what you do is physical. Your determination and fearless attitude of carrying out your action is your mental toughness.

"Practice makes perfect" should be changed into "Perfect practice makes perfect." Every practice is a practice of concentration.

All the information I have provided so far is based on the fact that the human is independent and the most intelligent being in the animal world. Humans have the most complete and sophisticated survival skills physically and mentally. Humans have the most complex and complete system to survive. Humans have the most powerful hand to carry out human intellectual programs.

Human intelligence and human capability still comes from human comprehension. Anything anybody can contribute will benefit human as a whole. I would like to propose a few mental and conceptual guidelines and encourage people to challenge the validity of these guidelines in the basic athletic mental training program.

C. Guidelines for Mental Training

1. *Mental* is what you think, know, see, and hear and how you feel.
2. *Physical* and *biomechanical* are what you do with your body.
3. What you know determines what you think. What you think determines what you do. Your eye tends to lead what you do. What you think with is your mind.
4. Thought initiates your action.
5. Your eye is the leader of your action. Action is blind.
6. What you think is the only thing that controls the eyes.
7. If you do not think, your eyes will take over the system.
8. Concentration is action specific.
9. Mental toughness is "If you think what is right, then do it decisively."

24

Philosophical Biomechanics

A. Why Philosophical Biomechanics?

Biomechanics is biomechanics. Why philosophical biomechanics? What is philosophical biomechanics anyway?

Biomechanics is a very important branch of science that studies the actions of the internal and external forces on the living body. It uses the basic principles in physics and mechanics to investigate the physical-mechanical problems related to life science. Using biomechanics properly could help a good runner running even faster. It could help a good swimmer swim even faster. It could help a good jumper jump even higher and farther. However, the human body is not a pure physical system; applying it properly is the key.

Tennis is a simple game, and it contains only a few athletic actions. All these actions are innate. That means through imitation and minor modification, everybody knows how to perform the actions in tennis. There have been so many past tennis champions in history. There are so many young good tennis players today. How many of them have accomplished what they have accomplished because they knew biomechanics? How many of them think biomechanics really helped them? If we ask all the good young tennis players today to see how many of them can explain what biomechanics is or let them explain how they use biomechanics in their game, you probably will be surprised of their answer.

I am not saying biomechanics is not important. What I am saying is that we have to take all the relevant information and explain it in humanistic terms to help athletes improve their performance.

People do not have to know biomechanics to play good tennis. However, it is proper and necessary to explain how the human body works and how different joints can help each other to avoid injury in the game of tennis. I have been in a few tennis conferences before, including the US tennis teachers' conferences. Each time, there is always a so-called expert in biomechanics giving a lecture on biomechanics. There is also a sports psychologist giving a lecture about psychology. It is disappointing that every time I leave with an empty feeling.

For sport psychology, I also feel something need to be done better in sport performance. It is my feeling that the sport psychologist should be the *mental instructor* for all athletes during the actual performance. *Mental*, in essence, is *psychological*. I am always wondering, if a sport psychologist tells a player exactly what the concentration mechanism is and tells the players precisely how to concentrate to perform, what other information do the players need to know to improve their performance? And what other information does a sport psychologist need to worry about and has not informed the players of yet? Because during the performance, the only thing the player needs to think about is how to concentrate to perform his/her specific action, and anything other than performing this specific action will become a distraction.

Some sport psychologists think to prepare an athlete to perform before the actual performance is important. They think they can prepare an athlete to be confident, to have a strong will to win. They think if an athlete can concentrate at *that moment*, the performance will be under perfect concentration. However, the mechanism of concentration is not that simple. Concentration has to be action specific; performing that specific action is the critical point for that concentration. Without the guidance of the sports psychologist to define the concentration precisely, the meaning of concentration is still not yet defined. Without proper concentration, an unforced error can happen easily. Once a player starts making a mistake, the confidence will promptly go. Then all the confidence built through hard times when the player was not playing is down the drain. Oftentimes, the word *concentration* can be wrongly defined. For example, if a coach tells his player, "I want you concentrate to win this point," winning is the result of the action; it is not the action. A strong desire to win does stimulate one's physical energy; at the same time, it can also be a serious distraction. Winning is a peripheral thought. It should not be the central thought. The player may be so eager to win and lose his sense of either mental or biomechanical concentration and end up as a loser.

The proper concentration on the hitting action mentally should be the *contact point* on hitting. The biomechanical concentration of the swing should be properly followed. The killing instinct is not proper if one does not know what the focal point of the concentration is. I think all the information should be provided to the athletes by a sports psychologist.

When a player makes a mistake on the court in tennis, he should be the one who knows exactly what happened and why. Learning to diagnose one's mistakes is the most important part of the training process.

Sports psychologists are different from sports trainers. They help athletes understand how the human system works related to sports performance. They guide athletes to think the right way. They lay everything sports-wise in the proper perspective. They provide a sound platform for athletes to develop and flourish.

Proper guidance and proper teaching is the foundation of the platform to progress. Confidence is built on proper performance. Good performance is built on proper concentration and execution of the actions. If there is confidence, there will be no fear. If there is no fear, there will be proper relaxation.

There were so many good players in the past. There are so many good tennis players today. Very few players play exactly the same way. Just like there are so many good fathers who raise good kids, very few do just exactly the same. Since we are all human, psychology must play an important role in that. Even we are not going to talk about the real biomechanics; however, the tennis players should understand the nature of the most common athletic actions. Since these actions are still biomechanical in nature, I propose the term *philosophical biomechanics*.

Philosophically speaking, the human body is like a family. Different joints are different members of that family. When something comes up, everyone participates and works together for a common goal. Each member has its own role to play. In the case of a real family, for example, Father drives to work, Mother does the cooking, the big brother helps the little brother go to school, and the little brother going to school. In this family, the principal job is for the little one going to school to study. The little one is the direct performing member. All other members in that family are the helpers. Everyone is doing his own job making sure the little one can accomplish his best.

Playing tennis is also like a family business. Your hand with the racket to hit the ball is like the little brother who is going to school in the previous example. Helping the hand to hit the ball is the main thing for the whole body. The hand is the direct performing member. The rest of the body is trying to help the hand to do its job. In order to hit the ball, you have to get there first. Then the catching action starts. When playing tennis, if you see the ball coming, your ankle moves, shifting your weight to initiate your movement. Your knee joint adjusts the height of your body vertically. Your hip joint adjusts your body position horizontally. Your shoulder adjusts the position of your elbow vertically and horizontally. Your elbow helps to position your wrist. Your wrist simply snaps the racket to hit the ball.

Let me repeat it. What I have described here previously is the essence of what the biomechanics in tennis really is. It is how the human body works in playing tennis. It is an automatic, centrally controlled, initiated-by-demand dynamic operational system. It is a sequential, rotational, and translational helping system. I want to repeat this. This is a sequential helping system. This is the most efficient way to adjust position and produce maximum dynamic hitting in playing sports. This is the best way to construct an artificial human (robot) to play the game.

In tennis, the hand is the direct performing member. It is the job of the hand to do. The hand just holds the racket, and the wrist manipulates and accelerate the racket to make the contact. This is the final step of a hitting action.

Usually, this is automatic in the human mind. The hitting action is a human survival skill. Everybody knows something about this. It is something you do, and you do not have to think too much about it. It is a part of our human nature. However, humans are different individuals. Some are born to be more athletic and work better biomechanically. Some need to be trained to be more efficient. This is the reason why biomechanics comes into the game of sports. This is the reason, I believe, we should explain how human body works athletically rather than use a lot of scientific jargon to confuse coaches and players.

The advantage of using the stepwise helping system to explain biomechanics is to prevent the load from causing shoulder injury. More shoulder involvement can prevent elbow injury, and more elbow involvement can prevent wrist injury and, more importantly, unnecessary sports injury. For example, more hip turns can prevent shoulder injury, more lower-extremity movements can prevent upper extremity injury in upper-extremity sports, and more upper-extremity movement can prevent lower-extremity injury in lower-extremity sports. Here, this is the main reason to keep whole body in dynamic balance during execution of athletic actions. This is the reason we have to talk about the upper athletic system and the lower athletic system as a whole unit.

In sports, biomechanics and psychology are inseparable. No matter what event you are performing, you have to know what you are doing, think about what you are doing, and do it. It involves what you think and what you do. What you do is biomechanical and what you think is psychological or mental. In sports, it is not you want to win and you win; it is not you do not want to fear and you will not be afraid. It is how you can concentrate properly and execute your action properly, and then you win. If you can concentrate, there will be no fear. This is the reason, I believe, sports psychologists should play a much wider role during psychological training for athletes in sport performance. The mechanism of *concentration* in mental and biomechanical part of sports actions should also be included in psychological training programs.

What I want to emphasize is that biomechanics and psychology are both important and necessary in terms of preventing injury and improving performance. Present many hip injuries, shoulder injuries, elbow injuries, and wrist injuries can be avoided from the stepwise helping biomechanical system. We can also explain how a 140 lb golfer can hit a golf ball farther than a strong 250 lb football player. However, the scope of application and degree of adaptation of biomechanics and psychology have to be critically selected. Since all human body movement is basically biomechanical in nature, we call this section philosophical biomechanics.

Biomechanics is no more than humans trying to use the basic physical principles to understand how the human body works mechanically and how to use this branch of science to help athletes to develop sport skills and prevent injury.

All these skills, biomechanical wise, in sports had already been demonstrated and performed practically by all the previous sports champions. How many previous Winboton champions knew biomechanics and been trained in sport psychology? How many green jersey winners in the golf US Open knew what biomechanics really is? That does not mean we should not try to understand and try to explain what people already know and should do what people have already done. The important thing is that we have to know exactly what we are doing. Our goal is to make people understand the game better and help people learn faster, to accomplish their goal easer and prevent injury.

I am not challenging whatever people have talked about in biomechanics, but I think people should think deeper and understand more about the game, both biomechanically and psychologically. The matter becomes more complicated because all the sports actions are part of our human nature, and our human nature complicates the performance of the sports actions. The fact of the matter is, understanding the games thoroughly is the very best way to help coaches to coach and to help players to play.

Historically, humans invented games similar to tennis hundreds of years ago. They all relate to the concept of hitting and throwing. Animals do what they can do to survive, and they use the skills to survive as games to play. Humans know how to hit and throw, so they can invent the game of hit and throw. The other animals play the games they can play. Usually, the games are their survival skills.

It is true that sport science is a branch of very complicated science. Scientific development in exercise physiology; design of new athletic equipment; sports medicine; and many other fields had contributed tremendously to the progress of modern sports. However, Biomechanics in tennis is still quite limited. It is not healthy and helpful to use a few scientific terms and a few Newtonian classic physical principles to describe tennis.

Tennis is a normal human activity, especially, the modern tennis game for human health. Describe tennis philosophically based on human physiology and mental understanding is the best way to help Coaches to coach and to help players to play.

B.   Understanding Ourselves

We are human. We are the most powerful and complicated biological machines on the earth surface. No living being can compete with humans except humans with human itself.

As humans, we have our commonalities. There are certain things in which we are all alike. There are certain things we are all different. However, there are so many things we can all do. We are all similar physiologically and anatomically but different genetically.

We can all run even though there are people who run faster. Not everybody can be a track star. We can all run for a long time, but not everyone can participate in a marathon. Running is just an event, but there are so many other physical and physiological conditions to determine that event.

We can all swing a baseball bat, but not everybody can play in the major league. We can all swing a tennis racket, but not everybody can play in the US Open. We can all swing a golf club, but not everybody can play like Tiger Woods.

What I am trying to say is that even though we are all alike, we are still different in many different areas. We may have some intrinsic physiological minor differences, and we may have some environmental and conditional differences. The important thing is that we are all human; we have many things in common. We all have the same survival skills. We all can learn and get better at the thing we can do. If you know something and you want to do, you can always get better if you practice more and really understand what you are doing because as humans, we have similar biomechanical features and equivalent intelligent potential better than any living animal on the earth's surface. Given the chances, the opportunity, and the supportive system, you have the ability to do probably anything anybody else can do. You can be good or better or the best, depending on whatever you choose and your physical condition, effort, and determination. You could be a genius or have a special talent not discovered yet. Humans often think humans know the best. In a general sense, it is true. Actually, humans are still a puzzle to humans themselves. We enjoy the earth provided for us. We play golf, we play tennis, we ski; we enjoy the sun, the wind, the mountain, and the sea. We, however, still try to figure where we came from. We may never know.

We are a perfect and magical biomechanical design. The biomechanical frame is simple, but to maintain the frame to work properly and to function continuously is very complicated. There are so many things we do not know about ourselves. This is the reason I am talking about the philosophical biomechanics.

As humans, we are a perfect balanced system. Do not let the words *balance* or *unbalance* scare you and confuse you. When you first started learning to walk, you learned the concept of balance already. The reason I mention the word *unbalance* is that many tennis and golf coaches complain that their students do not know how to balance themselves when the students make a tennis or golf swing. Usually, when this happens, in my mind, it is the miscommunication of the coach's part rather than the fault of the student.

A tennis swing is a very simple rotational motion. Even a forceful tennis swing can hardly cause unbalanced behavior. As coaches, you have to demonstrate a good swing motion with a proper center of rotation and let the students practice that motion repeatedly—many, many times. It is essential for the students to clearly feel the full swing motion. If the contact point is within the range of swing motion and there is no excessive improper extension at the point of contact, there should not be any sense of unbalance on the student's part.

Normally speaking, unbalance is a very good thing. Unbalance is the source of movement. When you move one foot forward and you create the unbalance, to balance this unbalance, it becomes your movement. Walking and running is a continuous balance-unbalance process. You automatically balance yourself for whatever you do normally. If you ever feel you are unbalanced when you are doing something such as swinging a golf club, swinging a tennis racket, swinging a baseball bat, or are on a ski slope or participating in any sport that involves hitting or throwing, you know you are making a mistake in controlling your body part when you are executing the specific action you are performing. That mistake is not because you do not know how to balance yourself. Your unbalance is caused by something you are not thinking about properly when you perform that action. Swinging in a hitting or throwing action is an overall rotational motion with multiple rotational and translational components. The center of rotation is within your biolink system. It can be a steady balanced rotational motion. It can also be a dynamic balanced rotational motion. It is a multirotational and multitranslational system in action. They are very complex, but they are self-coordinated and self-regulated and stay in dynamic balance during performance. This is part of the normal human dynamic movement. An important thing to keep balance is to have proper mental understanding of the action and to execute the action properly.

25

The Human Biolink System

The human biolink system is a centrally controlled initiated-on-demand, self-regulated, cooperative dynamic operational system. Before going to the specific joints, let's discuss the generality of the biolink system.

The human biolink system is the most intriguing one. The whole body's biolink system consists of the upper and lower biolink systems.

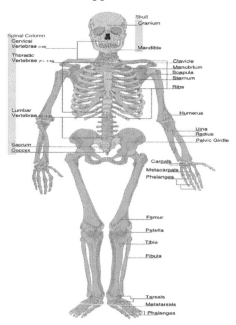

Figure 4

The human biolink system can be shown in figure 4. There are various segments of bones connected by different types of joints. The design of the human body is astonishing. It can use simple internal rotation of the sacrum to control and start the upper and lower power systems uniformly or separately. There are six long bones on the top, and there are six long bones at the bottom. Three bones each form two arms on the top, and three bones each form the two legs at the bottom. There are two single long bones each on the top with full rotational capability form the two upper arms and two single long bones each at the bottom with ball-and-socket joints at the bottom, forming the two upper legs. Most interestingly, two long bones each form the two forearm, and two long bones each form the two lower leg. The two long bones on the lower arms and the two long bones on the lower leg provide the pronation and supination of the wrist and ankle respectively. The number of bones of the wrist joint on the upper extremity and the number of bones on the ankle joint on the lower extremity enable the hands on the top and the feet on the bottom to perform multiple useful functions in the survival mechanism of the human race. Without the wrist joint structure, a human cannot manipulate tennis racket, golf club, or a baseball bat to play those games today. Without the wrist joint structure, a human could never throw anything like humans are throwing today.

The number of the bones and type of structures of a specific joint determine the degree of capability and type of functions that joint can perform. If we look at the human skeleton, as in figure 4, the hand and wrist have more bones than any part of the human body. The number of bones of a joint defines the complicity of the movement of that joint. That is the reason the human hand can perform all kinds of complicated functions. We can understand why the human hand is such a powerful organ.

The hand can hold an object as big as a baseball bat; it can also hold an object as small and thin as a needle. With the carpals, metacarpals, and phalanges, all the fingers can participate in all kinds of gripping functions. With the relative length of the fingers and the direction of extension of the fingers and the bony arrangement of the wrist with the neurological control, the hand becomes an almighty tool only humans can physiologically produce. The hand can hold almost any shape of objects and manipulate them in numberless ways. With the characteristics of the joints such as the carpals, metacarpals, and phalanges, the hands can play piano and all kinds of music instruments. Besides being the principal organ helping humans survive with the powerful hitting and throwing athletic actions, the hands help humans open the door to civilization. The hand is the most powerful hardware in the human neurological system.

There is nothing designed as beautifully and perfectly as the human body. The hip joint located in the middle provides the main power for both the upper and lower athletic system. For the upper athletic system, the hip joint is a helper and protector. For the lower athletic system, the hip joint is the initiator and power provider of all the lower-extremity movement.

The role the shoulder joint plays for the upper athletic system is the same as the role the hip joint plays for the lower athletic system athletically. The fine structure of the wrist and the ankle joint provides the capability of fine manipulation and controlled movements of the hand and the feet. The single long bones in the limb system simplify the mechanism of power transmission; the double long bone system is for the power and control of hands and the feet. The number of small bones in the wrist and ankle and the number of small bones in the hand and the feet are designed for the multiple functional manipulation and fine control.

In 2004, Harvard anthropologist Daniel Lieberman and University of Utah biologist Dennis Bramble jointly published a paper and stated that humans are born to run. Yes, I agree; however, running is just a very small part of what humans were born to do. Running is only the simplest part of the lower-extremity function. The lower-extremity system is not just for running, but it is also for jumping, kicking, and most importantly, it is designed to support the upper-extremity system.

I have proposed the concept that humans were born to hit and throw many years ago. I have emphasized that these physical and mental capabilities define what a human is. We also have a more complete picture now of how humans survived and what humans can do.

The human biolink system is powerful and delicate. The power of the upper link system comes from the degree of the freedom of rotation of the shoulder joint. Rotation of the shoulder joint creates the translation movement of the elbow joint; rotation of the elbow joint creates the translational movement of the wrist joint. The stepwise rotational translational mechanism is the most efficient mechanism to generate the maximum velocity at the end of the link system. Here, the end of the link is the wrist joint. The radial and the humerus long bones allow the wrist to create the most effective angular acceleration. The proper use of the wrist with the help of the elbow is the mechanism of making the most effective hitting and throwing action.

Here, I have to specially mention that understanding this section is the only way to avoid wrist injury and elbow injury. Please remember, the elbow supports your wrist; the shoulder supports your elbow. If the wrist and the elbow carry too much load by themselves, they can be damaged. Therefore, if a player's wrist hurts, let him use his elbow to reduce the load of his wrist, and if a player's elbow hurts, let him use his shoulder to help his elbow. Proper use of the helping system is the only way to avoid sports injury. There is another mental understanding we have to know in order to operate the biolink system properly and efficiently. For example, if one player has a sore elbow and we say he should use more of his shoulder, how should we tell him then? The answer is simple and mental. It is simply "When you make your swing, just think about using your shoulder more at contact."

Human system is a mutually beneficial comprehensible survival system. This is an ideal survival system. It requires all fractional parts in the whole system to work together, mutually dependable, mutually complimentary, and functionally idealistic to survive as an intact life.

Physiologically speaking, any life starts with two different kinds of life-creating ingredients, especially for complex life forms. Just one egg could not survive. Just one sperm could not survive. Unification of the sperm and egg is the beginning of a "whole" life. This is the common sense model of life creation.

Philosophically speaking, the mechanism of creation implies the necessity of a natural mechanism of survival in the purpose of creation. If a life is created for the purpose of not living, the creation does not have a purpose anymore. So humans must have a strong desire and good mechanism to survive.

As shown in figure 4, the skeleton shows that the human body has an upper half and a lower half. Human limbs have a right half and left half. The human brain has a right half and left half. The human system is designed as the most efficient and the most complete cooperative half-and-half survival system. The half-and-half concept is the simplest and most complete design mode. Both sides are not designed to be exactly the same in structure and function to avoid repetition. Even though some of them look very much the same, such as both arms and legs, they are mutually complementary, mutually beneficial, and mutually dependent. The human body is a wonderful two-parts-in-one mutually dependent and mutually beneficial common living body. How the whole body works—physiologically, anatomically, and psychologically—is defined as the complete human system.

Athletically speaking, the upper athletic system is designed specifically for swinging of both arms to create a complex defensive and offensive system physically or athletically. The equally designed two upper limbs are the ideal tools for carrying and holding of any object. The upper limbs are also the operating system for intellectual development.

We have defined the human system as a mutually dependable, categorical, supportive, and multifunctional twin-pack system. Just think, emotionally, from the difference between a one-arm hug and a two-armed hug among friends, a fight between a one-armed boxer and a two-armed boxer, we understand the difference, emotionally and physically, in the mechanisms of survival. When we listen to the difference in performance between a one-handed piano player and a two-handed piano player, we understand the real meaning of harmony and beauty in music. If we can think about how precisely our teeth in the upper jaw fit the teeth of our lower jaw, we will understand what a real complement means in human life. All in all, we should understand the true meaning of the complete human system.

Here, I want to recommend a book by Dr. Frank R. Wilson titled *The Hand and How Its Use Shapes the Brain, Language, and Human Culture.*

It is a wonderful collection of information of how the human hand has contributed to human culture and civilization.

I have stressed on the human hand structure previously, and I want to repeat it:

1. The power grip is one of the important hand functions, and it is responsible for the human to survive physically and historically. The power grip is the base for the physical actions of catching, punching, hitting, poking, slashing, and holding actions. The open hand is the base for the powerful actions of throwing, pushing, holding, and lifting.
2. The precision grip is the base for using tools and instruments and is the foundation of development of culture and civilization.

I also want to repeat that the most powerful action physically is still the action of throwing. The throwing action has the power and direction control build in our neurological system. The trajectory is imprinted in our brain, and the direction coincides with the extension of our forearm.

Now, once again, let's go back to the importance of the biolink system from the skeletal picture we have. The important objects are the two hands on the top and the two feet at the bottom. I am going to skip all the scientific terms anatomically because we are talking on the philosophical level and not on the anatomical level. You can see the hand has the most number of bony segments on the upper part of the body. The foot has the most number of bony segments and joints at the bottom. The number of the bony segments and joints represents the complexity of the types of movement of that bio body. So we can conclude that the foot and hand have the most complicated movements among our body parts. The hands are on the upper extremities, and the feet are on the lower extremities.

A. The Ankle Joint

The ankle joint is the most delicate and the most important part of the lower biolink system in my mind. The role the ankle joint plays in the lower biolink system is like the wrist to the upper biolink system. In the sense of pure physical survival, the wrist provides the hands with the functions of hitting and throwing actions.

Since the ankle is at the extreme position of the lower extremity system, it is the last responsible member of the lower extremity system in any lower extremity action. We can discuss the ankle function statically and dynamically.

Statically speaking, when the foot is firmly planted on the ground, it forms the base and support of the whole body. The balance of the whole body is determined by the fine movements of the ankle joint and determined by the fine movement of the whole body When the foot is firmly planted on the ground, the final lower joint itself performs the precision and control of the delicate movements of the foot in the action of kicking. We often observe soccer players perform their controlled kicking skills with all kinds of fancy movements. They kick the ball around their body with their feet almost like they throw the ball around their body with their hand. Without the proper ankle joint movement, they can never kick the ball like that.

It forms the base and support of the whole body. Rotational movements of the hips, limited allowable movements of the knees, and limited movements of the ankles together form the powerful lower-body biolink system. The ankle joint is responsible for the delicate proximal kicking movements as performed by some soccer players in ball control or when using kicking as a fighting skill in a boxing competition. The ankle joint is the primary performing member of the powerful kicking action in soccer or the kicking actions of a place kicker in football. The power is generated from the middle section of our body to initiate the lower biolink system; the ankle joint is responsible for directional control and point of contact in delivering the energy. The ankle joint at the lower extremity is the same as the wrist at the upper extremity; they play the role of directional control and direct impact in final execution of the action. When the lower biolink system is activated, it usually starts from hip rotation to knee flexion down to ankle participation to direct the foot action. The upper body movement is totally geared to help and enhance the delivering the energy generated by the lower biolink system. Without proper ankle movement, humans can never run, jump, or kick as humans do.

The ankle joint is a hinged synovial joint with basic up-and-down movement (plantar flexion and dorsiflexion). However, when the range of motion of the ankle and the subtalar joint are taken together, the complex function is as a universal joint. We can see how complicated the joint movement is. In order to make things easier, we can call them all rotational joints. The reason I prefer to call them rotational joints is because they function as a unit but they still remain in their original place. If we choose to draw a line at any joint in any direction at a specific plane, we can classify that joint movement as rotational. At the end of the other bony joint, it will become a translational movement.

Even though we are talking about the ankle joint, we have to know that the ankle joint is only a part of the lower biolink system. The ankle joint, the knee joint, and the hip joint all together form the total lower biolink system. We cannot move any single joint without activating the other joints in the whole lower biolink system.

B.   The Knee Joint

Since the biolink system is so important in understanding the entirety of body mechanics in athletic performance, I am going to say it repeatedly. The reason I named it the biolink system is to differentiate it from the common physical link system. The neurologically controlled link system is very different from the purely mechanical link system. The biolink system is stepwise controlled and completely synchronized. Please remember, though, the biolink system is only part of the total body. It is only designed as the most efficient mechanism to enable humans to survive in the ecological system.

In terms of athletic performance, the human body is like a family. Every joint is like a single member of the entire family. It is the whole family's job to face any challenge dynamically. In general, there is a specific part of the body directly called for to act. Usually, the member at the end of the chain is the direct performer. For example, in kicking, running, and jumping, it is the foot; in hitting and throwing, it is the hand. However, the rest of the body is already informed and well prepared to help whatever needs to be done to help the foot in kicking and to help the hand in hitting or throwing. The special feature of the biolink system is to use this stepwise rotational translational feature to help the foot in kicking and to help the hand in hitting or throwing. The function of the biolink system is to help the foot and hand reach the location of contact and accelerate the foot in a kicking action and help the hand to reach and accelerate the hand in a hitting or a throwing action. This system is ingrained in our neurological system. It is a part of our brain tissue. It is a part of our life. It works naturally when we are performing an athletic activity. If we do things right, there is an effective kicking or hitting action and no injury of our lower athletic system in kicking, and there will be no injury of our upper athletic system in hitting. The whole body is in an absolutely cooperative mode at all times.

Every single athletic action is like the whole family trying to perform one specific job; if everyone knows what his role is and just does his own job, the result of this work will be well done. If any single member wants to do more, he may be overloaded and get hurt. This biolink system will tell which member of the family can get help from which member of this family.

As seen from the human skeletal structure, as in figure 4, for every long bony segment, both ends must be involved in the joint relationship. The knee joint is in between the long bone femur on the top and tibia at the bottom. If the knee makes a movement without changing its location, the ankle will make a bigger movement and change its location from one place to another. Some people may call this the knee flexion. As I mentioned earlier, we call this knee rotation and ankle translation.

The sequential rotational translational system is the simplest and most efficient mechanical design for acceleration and efficiency. It is the most intriguing arrangement of the limbs system to generate power in the hitting and throwing actions. It also serves as the distance adjustment of reaching in the catching and grabbing action. The mechanism of eye-hand coordination depends on the extension of our limbs to reach a specific location. This wonderful design has enabled humans to survive in an unfriendly environment since the ancient times.

The knee plays a double role in both upper and lower athletic systems. In the lower athletic system, hip rotation creates displacement of the knee joint. Here, the knee joint is an important member of the lower athletic system. It helps to generate power and velocity of the ankle joint in kicking, running, and jumping actions. We can simply say that the hip rotation is to produce the knee translation and the knee rotation to produce the ankle translation. These sequential rotation and translation make up the powerful lower biolink system in all the lower-extremity athletic performances. Therefore, the knee joint is the most important and active member of the active lower athletic system.

In terms of upper-extremity athletic performances such as hitting and throwing actions, the knee joint plays a role in facilitating the hip movement and motivating the whole upper athletic system (from the hip up) to make a hitting, throwing, or catching action. Practically speaking, the time and location of the upper extremity system depends entirely on the support of the lower Extremity system. The knee joint and the ankle joint are the parts of the body that change the location or the vertical position of the entire upper biolink system. Therefore, proper knee movement is critical for upper extremity performance. For example, during serve in tennis, people tend to bend their upper body instead of using their knee bend. A tennis player may get hurt if not using the knee properly. In a golf swing, people should lock their knee joint in a horizontal position during the takeoff and the down swing in order to ensure proper contact. Important points for us to understand is that the knee is the important joint to adjust the vertical position of our upper biolink system and is the accelerating joint in our lower athletic movement either horizontally and vertically. The function of the knee is controlled by the hip joint. This is the function of the single long-bone femur. The function of the ankle joint at the end of the tibia and fibula is controlled by the joint of the knee. The mechanism of concentration to control the knee in a golf swing is to think of the knee during the takeoff and the down swing.

The anatomical structure of the knee is not very complicated. When I say rotation of one joint creates a translational movement of the next joint, rotation of the next joint will create a translational movement of the one next to the next joint. It is a sequential stepwise rotation and translational chain. This is really a simplified statement. Let me try to explain a little here again using the knee joint.

The knee joint is typically a hinge joint. The fibular collateral ligament and the posterior part of the tibial collateral ligament are made tight by extension of the knee and relaxed by flexion. The anterior part of the tibial collateral ligament remains tense in all positions of the knee. The two ligaments together restrain rotation of lateral movement of the knee, especially in the extended position. That is why everybody knows that knee joint cannot rotate. However, if we arbitrarily draw a line from the left to right through the center of the knee joint, this hinge joint will be rotating against that line, when we extend our knee. For simplicity reason, to understand the situation when we move our knee slightly, our ankle will move a much longer distance; that is why we can say that the knee rotation (extension if you will) will create translational movement of the ankle. This is the reason I propose the sequential stepwise rotational translational biolink system. This particularly mentioned stepwise rotational translational system works both in upper and lower athletic systems. We all know that this is how human limbs generates power in athletic movement. In our lower athletic system, we have our tibia and fibula. We have the knee on the top, and we have the ankle at the bottom. Once our hip rotates, it starts the dynamic chain down to the knee and to the ankle. This is the reason the kicking action is so powerful. The power of the kicking originates from the hip joint.

Our forearm, for example—on one side is the elbow and on the lower side is the wrist. For our tibia and fibula, we have the knee on the top and the ankle at the bottom. For example, if we simply flex our arm, the elbow is a hinge joint. It allows the movement only in one direction. However, if we draw a line perpendicular to the upper arm and perpendicular to the direction of flexion, then this flexion becomes a rotation. If we simplify the joint movement, it will be much easier to explain body mechanics in a future discussion. For example, if I put my arm straight on the surface of a table with my hand face up and flex my forearm, my elbow will be rotating against the line parallel to the table surface and perpendicular to my extended arm and extending through my elbow joint. Then, I can interpret this situation as the following:

when my elbow makes a rotation, my wrist will make a translation. When the sacrum makes a rotation, the knee will make a translation. Here it simply means, when the sacrum makes a movement without changing its location, the knee will make a movement and change its location. It could be up or down or it could be left or right.

C. The Hip Base and the Hip Joint

Before I say anything else, I just want to remind the readers that the hip base and the hip joints are the most important parts of our body in terms of what we can do athletically in our lives. It is the center of initiation of the dynamic movement of all the biolink systems. Since human body is a dynamic balance system, the total dynamic balance also depends on the movement of the hip Base and hip joint.

The pelvis is a bony structure formed by the innominate bones, the sacrum, and the coccyx and are united together by ligaments. This structure serves as the support of the vertebral column and for articulation with the lower limb. The hip joints are the connectors, supporters, and movement generators of the upper part of the body as well as the lower part of the body. And it is the dynamic stabilizer in keeping the whole body in balance statically. It is also the central area and responsible for the initiation of movement of both the upper and the lower biolink system. The movement of the hip base and the hip joint is the primary mechanism to maintain dynamic balance of the whole body.

The hip joint is the most powerful joint in the biolink system. There are eight groups of muscles that can be used as external rotators. Seven groups of muscles can be used as internal rotators. Five groups of muscles can be used as extensors. Eight groups of muscles can be used as flexors, and five groups each as abductors and adductors. The hip base complex provides power and precision in managing and support the upper and lower biolink system.

The hip joint plays different roles for upper and lower parts of the biolink system. The hip complex is the powerhouse of the human skeletal system. Hip rotation is the primary movement to change the direction of the whole skeletal system. The concentration mechanism of catching in tennis, soccer, or any other athletic activities is to think about the *hip*, not the *feet*, even though people used to call it the footwork.

In the upper biolink system, hip rotation creates translational movement of the shoulder, rotational movement of the shoulder creates translational motion of the elbow, rotational movement of the elbow creates translational motion of the wrist, and rotational movement of the wrist creates directional change and controls the action specifically performed by the *hand*. This action can be either a hitting action, a throwing action, or any other action specifically performed by the hand.

Here, let me repeat it. I call the human body a rotational and translational system, which is making a very big simplification. For athletic performance, we just want to make it as simple as possible, and all we are doing is part of our physiological system; we naturally know what we are doing and we know how to do it. Otherwise, it will be too complicated for people to read about. For example, for the synovial joints, there are basically three types: unilateral (rotate only about one axis), biaxial joints (movement about two perpendicular axes), and multi-axial joints (movement about three perpendicular axes). They are the hinge joint, pivot joint, condyloid joint, saddle joint, ball-and-socket joint, and plane joint. For simplicity, I just call all of them the rotational joint because from the gross structure of any joint, we can draw a line through the center of that joint and interpret that movement as rotation. If we fix the location of that joint as a rotational joint, then the joints at the other end of this long bone will be the translational movement.

Now let me repeat this. If you just turn your hip base slightly in a sitting position (either your right or your left hip), your shoulder will move a distance of an arc. By the same token, if you stand or sit at one position, just swing or move your arm without moving your body position; you will find that the shoulder just rotates and your elbow will move a distance according to your will. That is what I mean by saying the shoulder rotation will create elbow translation. In the same manner, the rotation of the elbow will produce translational movement of the wrist. The wrist is the control joint of the hand to perform all kinds of jobs. This is the stepwise rotation and translational mechanism to control the end of the biolink chain. This is the most effective way to create variable velocity at the end of the chain. It is also the ideal control mechanism of the final member of the biolink system. This is the way wherein by slightly moving our shoulder, we can put our hand in a thousand different positions around our body.

In the lower biolink system, rotation of the hip creates translational movement of the knee, rotational movement of the knee creates translational movement of the ankle, and movement of ankle determines the direction of what the foot is going to do in this biolink system. This could be running, jumping, kicking, or any other direction specifically performed by the feet.

The hip joint plays a dual role in athletic performance. It can start the upper biolink system chain if the level of performance is required. It can start the lower athletic system if the performance demands it. It is the powerhouse of the human body movement horizontally. By the same token, the knee joint is the powerhouse of the human body movement in the vertical direction.

It is also important to mention that the human body is a system of totality. There is central neurological control of all the movements. If any part of the body needs to perform a specific action, the rest of the body will play the role as helpers to cooperate and assist to help accomplish that action. All the actions are self-coordinated, synchronized and controlled by the central nerve system if they are not interfered with neurologically. The interferences are usually any idea other than the performance of that specific action.

The most important work for athletic coaches and teachers in tennis, golf, and other athletic actions is to help players to define a proper efficient action and let the players to perform that action repeatedly until that action becomes a part of the player's system. For example, for golfers, to establish his/her own consistent mental swing; for tennis players, to establish his/her consistent mental swing; for soccer players, to establish his/her consistent mental kicking action. This is the best way to practice the mechanism of concentration. This is the best way to improve an athlete's performance.

Now, let's us think again about the word *concentration*. From *Webster's Dictionary*, *concentration* is the act or process of concentrating; the state of being concentrated; paying exclusive attention to one object. We have talked about concentration for so much and so long. We have mentioned this process many times before. We already know that it is a mental process. However, because it is so important and it is the centerpiece of our discussion, we will talk about it again and again.

How do we really concentrate then? We can follow the definition of it being a mental process. Concentration is to think about the action, the object, the matter, the process in which you are interested in exclusively. It is a mental process. It is a thought process. Thought initiates action. You do what you think. You do what you want to do. What you think and want are mental. To think is also a part of the concentration process. Here, let me give an example. Skiing is a lower-extremity sport activity. When we go skiing, we look at the white snow. We see everything in sight. We think how we did last time; we think many things not related critically to what under our feet. The concentration process should be as follows: (1) what is the action involved and (2) how our body should execute. In this case, skiing is a lower-extremity sport. Our concentration is on our lower extremity. The upper extremity mainly helps the lower extremity and should be relaxed to follow our thoughts of the hip motion. Here, of course, I am not talking about the high-level skier. High-level skiers just take off because they know what they should be doing already. For them, concentration is automatic. Just like a good tennis player who just goes and hit the ball on the tennis court. Here, what we are talking about is the concentration process and how one can learn the concentration process and make the concentration become his/her own system. An important thing to remember is that concentration is about a specific action. Thinking about the action only mentally and executing that action properly with appropriate biomechanical movement physically is the complete process of concentration.

Concentration is a process. One learns and one forgets. Interferences come in so easy and so often, especially the intellectual interferences, because it is the intellectual way for us to think about the thing we do. Through intellectual reasoning and thinking intuitively, we often miss some in-depth scientific understanding of the physical nature of the action and the physiological principles of the human body. We often feel that it is the right way to do. For example, when we talk about the footwork in tennis, we feel that we should think about moving our feet. Actually, thinking about moving our feet will delay the feet movement. This reasoning seems right intuitively. However, it is not the proper way in terms of the catch concentration. The proper catching concentration should be just thinking of getting there and constantly moving your hip base. Most of the time, it is not because we don't think; it is because we think too much and we think too many things that are not associated with the concentration mechanism at all.

Concentration is not just a process; it is an active process packed with all kinds of physical and mental activities. It could be an active action in tennis, golf, or any other sports. In this case, concentration becomes critical. Then, to prevent any new interference with the player's performance mentally or biomechanically should be the coaches' ongoing effort. Most of the time, the interference comes from an unnecessary mental thought. That thought compromises the proper thought of the action itself. The simplest examples in tennis and golf are like these: I want to win this point. I want to hit hard. I cannot miss this point. I want to play safe. If I keep playing like this, I will win.

What I am trying to say is that anything you think of is not directly related to the execution of the action; it may very well interfere with the execution of that action. If any thought is not directly associated with the execution of that action, you should not think about it. You should be clearly aware that the time of your performance is very short. Concentration on the action is your choice.

We have described the lower athletic system from the ankle up to the hip base. If there is a need for a kicking action, this information will be processed through our brain and start the kicking action. For all parts of our lower biolink system, the movement starts from our hip base and extends to the knees and the feet.

For a kicking action, the hip joints are the primary movers. The point of contact and the direction of the kicking is controlled by the ankle; the power of the kicking comes from the hip joints. The whole upper athletic system is used to balance and facilitate the execution of the kicking action by the lower athletic system.

D. The Shoulder Joint

The amazing thing about the human system is that there are numerous different systems that all work in their own way for different purposes. All the systems are mutually beneficial and mutually dependent with a common goal of a healthy and prosperous life.

The hip joint is the primary mover of the lower athletic system in walking, running, jumping, and kicking; it is also the primary supportive mechanism of the upper athletic system. All these functions are the contributions of the strong ball-and-socket joint.

The shoulder joint is quite different. The shoulder joint is not a ball-and-socket joint. It is a sternoclavicular joint. It contains two synovial cavities, which are separated by a fibrocartilaginous articular disk. The adjacent surfaces of the clavicle and sternum do not fit too well together. This structure allows the joint to move somehow like the ball-and-socket joint so the shoulder can perform up-and-down, forward-and-backward, and free rotational movements. In an up-and-down motion, which is the easiest, the clavicle moves on the disk as on a hinge. For other movements, the disk moves with the clavicle. The joint also include a portion of the first rib as it attaches the sternum of the chest.

The shoulder blade is called the scapula. The scapula is a big triangular bone on top of our back. This triangular bone has three borders. There are superior, medial, and lateral. The surface of the scapula is relatively smooth. The dorsal surface is divided into two parts by the projecting spine. The area above the spine is the supraspinatous fossa and below the spine is called the infraspinatous fossa. The costal surface is called the subscapular fossa. These fossae are occupied by muscle of the same name as the fossae. The scapulae are suspended by muscles. The only articulations of the scapula are with the humerus of the arm and the clavicle.

In general, when we talk about the shoulder in tennis, we normally just think about the top of the humerus and the top of our armpit. That is the region between the arm and the body. Actually, in human anatomy, the shoulder region covers the breast pectoral region, the region of the back around the shoulder blade and the armpit. The shoulder muscles cover the upper part of the chest and spread backward and completely cover the true back muscles. Upon close examination of the shoulder, the muscular coverage includes much of the trunk and an upper part of the arm. So we can tell how important the shoulder is to our human activity.

The shoulder is the most powerful joint of the human upper body. It is the primary mover and the final support of the upper-extremity athletic activities. The shoulder to the arm is like the hip to the leg in sport performance. However, the neurological and muscular arrangements are quite different. It shows what our feet can do or what our hands can do in our lives. With the shoulder joint moving even more freely than a ball-and-socket joint and a powerful lower biolink system, we can understand the advantage of humans over other primates.

Spcaking from the biolink perspective, any movement of the shoulder will produce a translational movement of the elbow as well as the wrist joint. Since the shoulder simply hangs in the girdle and is surrounded by muscles all around, its movement is so easy and comfortable it makes the hand use so convenient and powerful.

The position of the shoulder can be adjusted vertically by bending the knee. The direction of the use of the shoulder can be adjusted through turning of the hip. Proper use of the shoulder becomes the most important part of the upper extremity sports.

We have mentioned that the human body is like a family. Any sport activity requires whole-body participation. Sports-related activities like boxing, baseball pitching, tennis serving, and weight lifting can demonstrate how powerful and diversified the function of the shoulder joint is. Not like the hip joint, the shoulder joints are support by all the strong muscles around the shoulder and the upper part of the chest and the back. It clearly demonstrates the importance of the upper body athletic system. No matter how strong one joint is, it is always under the risk of possible injury. Injury prevention is also one of the principal reasons this book is written.

1. What does the shoulder joint mean in tennis strokes? Since we know tennis is an upper-extremity sport, we can understand what an important function the shoulder joint plays in the game of tennis. A full shoulder turn in backward swing motion represents the maximum degree of preparation for any possible tennis hitting action. A fast-forward swing with your mind on the shoulder joint means the maximum deliberation of a tennis hitting action.

2. Everybody has one full tennis swing.

You do not have to learn it, but you have to practice it. Just like I mentioned previously, all the joints in the biolink system are similar to the members in the whole family. The tennis stroke development requires all members in the family or all the joints in the shoulder system to participate. All the members of the upper biolink system participating does not mean every stroke has to hit with full strength. Just like a family wants to go to a picnic or a family wants to go to lift a car from a ditch, how hard we want to hit the ball is determined by the mind. In the upper biolink system, the wrist is the direct performing member. All other joints in the upper biolink system just try to help the wrist to accomplish its job. If we think the shoulder is the master of the house, the lower biolink system (from the hip down) is just like the transportation the family has in doing the family job.

3. The shoulder is the most powerful joint in the upper biolink system.

It is also the final member that all other members depend on. The whole arm is a closely linked family system. There is no turning or moving of other joints; the shoulder joint is not felt. Of course, in any full tennis stroke, before the shoulder's full participation, we have to have the wrist and elbow well prepared before the full shoulder turning takes place. Turning of the upper biolink system is in the order of reverse direction in the back swing and the forward swing. During the stroke preparation, the order of turning is the wrist, the elbow, and then the shoulder. During the forward swing, the order is the shoulder, the elbow, and the wrist. The wrist is the last joint making the final contact and delivering the maximum acceleration of the head of the racket. Remember, though, the wrist simply delivers the physical movement of the racket, and the practical hitting is still the burden of the whole arm. Here I did not emphasize the turning of the hip joint because the hip certainly will make the necessary turn before the shoulder tries to do its job.

4. *Follow through* is used as a term to describe the racket movement after the contact until the end of the racket swing motion.

We have mentioned that in the concept of mental understanding and mental concentration, our mind is concentrated on the action. Here, the action is the swing. The swing is the movement of the hip, the shoulder, the elbow, and the wrist. Therefore, the term *follow through* should be the relative movement of all the joints that are used to help or to back up the wrist movement. Wherever the wrist goes, all the other joints of the arm should follow. For a forceful tennis stroke, the follow through will end up with a full shoulder swing motion. We can tentatively say that a full follow through is a full shoulder turn after the initial contact. Some strokes do not need a full shoulder turn, so the follow through will be different for different strokes. Here I have to point out that during preparation of the tennis swing, the hip movement is also important. There is also backward and forward movement of the hip joint. However, we have to think the hip joint is simply to prepare for the upper biolink system. If the hip moves a certain degree backward to prepare the upper body, it will turn the same way forward during the forward swing of the upper body. If the hip joint turns more during the forward swing, it will cause unbalance and create interference of the stroke. In conclusion of the shoulder joint, let me repeat it. The degree of the final shoulder position determines how hard you want to hit the ball. The hip joint is the big helper of the upper biolink system. The hip turning helps in adjusting the shoulder position horizontally. The knee movements help in adjusting the shoulder position vertically. A full shoulder forward turn means a full follow through.

E. The Elbow Joint

The elbow joint is the principal supporter for all the tennis strokes. From our previous skeletal picture, we know that there is a single long bone from the shoulder down to the elbow. This long bone is called the humerus. And then there are two long bones from the elbow down to the wrist. Flexion and extension of the elbow involves the single long bone of the upper arm and the two long bones of the lower arm at the same time without relative movement of the two long bones of the lower forearm. What I am trying to say is that flexion and extension of the elbow joint occurs between the humerus and both the ulna and the radius while pronation and supination involves rotation of the radius about the ulna. This is the reason the wrist joint has the mobility of doing the things the wrist can do. Only the two long bones in the skeletal system of the lower arm and the two long bones of the lower leg's skeletal system can provide this kind of mechanism. Remember, though, I did call this flexion and extension as rotation because we are looking at the gross movement of the arm at the elbow joint with an arbitrary axis of rotation. The purpose is to try to simplify the interpretation of the relative movement of the biolink system. A slight rotational movement of the radius about the ulna in pronation and supination will produce a considerable translational movement of the wrist joint.

A tennis stroke is an automatic biomechanical swing. Everybody can do it.

The best way to teach is to make a demonstration of the swing. The shoulder is the primary mover of the upper biolink system. The elbow is the operator of all the tennis strokes. The wrist is the member that delivers the strike upon contact. The shoulder constantly pushes the elbow joint forward to do whatever the whole arm is supposed to do. If you have played tennis for a long time, you do not even feel what you are doing with your swing. You simply run to the ball and hit the ball with whatever is on your mind at the time. However, if you consciously pay attention to what you are doing, you can sense how and what your shoulder and your elbow are doing in your swing. I personally feel this is the best way to understand what we are doing before we do it. Otherwise, when we get a bad habit, we do not even know we have a bad habit. We think when we are doing something, but we may not really be doing what we think we are doing. We sometimes feel that we know which part of our body is doing what; however, in reality, our body is not doing what we think it is doing. Of course, sometimes it could be just misinterpretation or misconception. I have seen some coaches explain their biolink system with a swing. Their explanation did not fit in with their body movements. We have to use the precise terms to describe the body movement in stroke production; otherwise, it will cause big confusion. In either case, the best way to understand what we are doing is to check the result of our effort and the method we are using. If we do the best we can and keep practicing what we understand the best way we can, this is the shortest way for any tennis player to reach his goal. This is why I advocate the concept of mental understanding and concentration.

The elbow is the primary joint for the pronation system of the forearm. Of course, the pronation starts from the shoulder down. Let's use layman's terms to describe pronation and supination. Pronation is simply the action done at any time you want to see the back of your hand. The action of turning your hand to show your palm is called supination. In the same way, the action of turning your hand to see the back of your hand is called pronation.

There are another two actions of the wrist that are also very important in terms of hand function. We call this wrist deviation. It is like if you put your hand at a neutral position—that is, you do not see either palm of your hand and the back of your hand. At that position, you can drop or raise your wrist. If you drop your wrist, it is called ulnar deviation. If you try to raise your hand up, this is called radial deviation. If you try it, you will find that the ulnar deviation is much easier, and it is about twice as big as the radial deviation. The pronation, supination, ulnar, and radial deviation allow humans to do the things that the other primates cannot do.

The pronation system is very important in athletic performance. This pronation system controls the power and direction of the hitting and throwing actions. It is the rotation of the shoulder that pushes forward the elbow joint. The elbow joint pronates to place the wrist joint in the proper place and direction, with a ready laid-back wrist to deliver the planned action. This is an automatic action in the human mind. It, however, requires practice to become more efficient.

In general, when we pronate our wrist, it is the result of the elbow pronation. However, there is a big difference if we think about wrist pronation or elbow pronation. In tennis strokes, there are certain strokes wherein we just emphasize the wrist function, and there are other strokes wherein we need more elbow action. Also for some strokes, we need primarily shoulder action. In order to practice all these strokes, we have to understand the mental part of the game. The mental part of the game is what our body is doing, but actually it is not what it is working on. This is the reason I specially emphasize the word *concentration*. The simplest way is we have to think about the shoulder pushing the elbow forward to practice the shoulder function. We have to think about the elbow performing the pronation action. We have to make the wrist acceleration as an automatic deliberation action. The mechanism of concentration is to put your mind (think) on the specific joint if you want to use or practice that joint. Keep practicing until your understanding becomes part of your natural movement, then your stroke will be automatic. If you want to hit the ball harder, think about your shoulder more and turn your shoulder faster. If you want to put more spin, think about pronating your elbow faster. Keep your wrist action as a constant delivery system. Actually, your wrist and your elbow turn about the same time.

The reason I want to emphasize so much here is this is the critical stage for you to develop your stroke with the concentration mechanism together as a unit.

F. Wrist Joint

We have mentioned this many times before: playing tennis is like a family job for the human body. Every joint in the body is a member of this family. We have also mentioned that when the lower extremity performs its job, such as kicking or jumping, the upper extremity plays the assistant role. When the upper extremity performs its job, such as hitting or throwing, in tennis and golf, the lower extremity play the role as an assistant. If the job is light, only some of the family members participate. If the job is heavy, everybody in the family participates. Sometimes, even when a member is not participating, it does not mean it is not aware or not ready to participate. For example, if you just want to do something with your wrist or your finger, you can feel that your shoulder will have muscle activity. Family members are linked together through kinship; the biolink system members are linked together through neurological system. The human body is a very tightly bound family.

The wrist function plays the most important role in the upper biolink system. The wrist is the joint that controls the hand function. It is the joint that controls the contact on hitting. It is the joint that controls the direction of hitting and throwing in all the upper-extremity sports actions. It is the joint that provides the maximum angular acceleration of any implement held by the hand. It has the fast angular acceleration in releasing of the throwing action. It is responsible for creating the fastest club head speed in golf and fast racket head speed in tennis. All other joints play a helping role to help the wrist controlling the hand to accomplish its job. The wrist together with the hand is the direct performer of all the actions of upper-extremity sports. The purpose is to snap the wrist from the laid-back position to the full pronated and extended position in a hitting or a throwing action. The pronation happens at both ends of the two long bones of the forearm. The pronation action of the hand will align the direction of releasing in the throwing action with the forearm. The elbow joint works together with the wrist joint as a unit. It is the elbow joint that helps and supports the wrist function. The internal rotation of the shoulder serves as a secondary backup mechanism to push the elbow to the proper position in time for the hand to do its job. The hip joint serves as the vehicle to transport the upper biolink system to the proper location to perform its job.

There is one thing very important here in tennis hitting. No matter what stroke you use, at the time of contact, your racket contacts the back of the ball with a certain degree of openness of the racket facing the direction where you want the ball to go. This is the fact of pure, simple physics. However, there is a huge mental problem here. The problem is, if you pay too much attention to the ball, it is very hard not to think where you want the ball to go. Once you think where you want the ball to go, your swing tends to follow the trajectory of the ball fly. This thought will compromise the effectiveness of your swing. All these thoughts are part of the throwing concept. All these thoughts are not helpful when the action of hitting is required. This is the conflicting part of the concept of hitting and throwing. The proper concentration should be only on contacting the ball without worrying about placement of the ball. However, these concepts are all in our brain, and this is the part of our intellectual ability. And we are born this way. On the contrary, if we do not think this way, it will be a serious problem for us as humans. We can say the devil of the mental problems is the ball. However, we should not blame the ball. The real problem is still our being human. It is still because we know too much; we are too smart and we think too much. We know anything we want to do ahead of time. We tend to anticipate the results of any action we do. This is why I call this intellectual interference. However, we should be much smarter than people think we are. We should not let all these affect our hitting concept. We should know that all these thoughts are not actions themselves. We should concentrate on the actions. The actions are catching, hitting. When we see the ball, we know already what we want to do with the ball. We already know what we want to accomplish. At the same time, we can see what is going on at other side of the court, and we know where is preferable for the ball to go, and then here comes the ball. This is all the information we receive from our eyes all the time. We run to intercept the ball. The thought of "getting there" is only less than a split second, then we have to strike at the ball. The concentration switches from catching to hitting almost immediately, especially when the ball is coming very fast. This seems like a process of preparing to hit and hit. We have to think critically about the concentration of hitting. This hitting process includes the speed of the coming ball and the readiness to make the contact. When we make the swing, the tendency is to use the swing, making the ball go to the target area and to make your opponent miss his shot. There is no intelligent person that does not want this happen. Then we tend to think too much again. Also during the action, the wrist is the joint of our upper biolink system to perform this job. The human intellectual mind orders the hand to do this job. The sense of direction of the ball fly becomes the mental interference problem of the wrist's proper pronation. That is why we see some players make a forehand swing without any pronation action at contact. This intellectual thought prevents the wrist from moving smoothly in the upper biolink system. I call this delayed wrist pronation syndrome. The best way to correct this problem is to make a fast wrist movement during the contact. We have to switch our mind from where we want the ball to go to a fast wrist flexion and pronation action.

Mind switch training is a necessary method in tennis education. The mind switch usually goes together with eye movement. It is simply how smoothly and fast you can change your thought from one thing to another as fast as possible decisively. Proper thought process and mind switching is at the center of mental tennis training program. It simply tells the players when to think what. Mind switching is absolutely necessary in playing the game of tennis, and it is often accompanied with the change of visual field. This visual field change often relates to switching from attention to focus and vice versa. When playing tennis, we have to change our mind from one thing to another at all times. If we know very well how to perform one action and we do it well all the time, then we do not even to think about it when we do it, and it becomes a part of our system. This is the best situation we want to be in as a good athlete in any sport. When you get to that degree of efficiency, the mind switch and mind training will not be needed anymore. If you could be like that on all your tennis strokes, you would be the top player right now. To reach this kind of efficiency requires numberless repetition of the specific actions. This is the reason any good athlete has to devote years of hard work to practice to reach a high degree of efficiency.

26

Summarization of the Biolink System

The reason I propose the biolink system is to try to simplify the conventional biomechanics lectures some sports scientists give in some sport meetings. I want to make the biomechanical movements of our body as simple as possible to understand what we are and how we can take advantage of our anatomical feature when we play sports. The biolink system does not aim to replace the biomechanics lectures in major academic institutions.

We all have similar anatomy. We all know when and how our joints work and why. I just want to point out that group participation in a specific job is better as long as each individual member performs its own assignment. This cooperation can prevent another joint from being overburdened and getting injury. This is the reason I said the hip joint, shoulder, elbow joint, wrist joint, knee joint, and ankle joint are one big family. There is one on the top, the hand. There is one at the bottom, the foot. Everything else is in the middle. All the joints in the middle, between the hands and the feet, are assigned to help the hands and feet perform three things: (1) to reach a certain spot in time to make the contact (the catching action of the hand and the foot); (2) to deliver the proper maximum energy inwardly in a specific direction (the hitting, rotational, swing motion); and (3) to deliver the maximum energy outwardly in a specific direction (the rotational motion in the throwing action and the kicking action). I want to emphasize it again that the end of the chain is the primary working member of the whole biolink system. All other joints are the principal supporters. They work together, and they help one another continuously in a stepwise fashion.

I also have to remind the readers that here, we are talking about the sport. The sport uses the major joints of the biolink system. The major joints are the hip, the knee, and the ankle in the lower biolink system, and they are the shoulder, the elbow, and wrist in the upper biolink system. The minor joints in the biolink system are the joints in the fingers and the toes. The minor joints in the hand structure play the principal roles in the invention of tools and the development of civilization and arts and music. Without the anatomic structure of the minor joints, there will be no piano playing and penmanship writing and drawing.

The biolink system is the essence of what humans are in terms of survival in athletics. The design of the biolink system is absolutely amazing. Every action starts from the center of the power point, the hip. In the human system, the hip joint initiates both the upper and lower athletic actions to begin with for any intended action. The hip rotation creates translational movement of the shoulder. The shoulder rotation produces translational movement of the elbow. The rotational movement of the elbow creates translational movement of the wrist. This is the series of the upper-extremity athletic movement in any action. This series of movement takes the hand to the location to perform its job. The lower-extremity athletic movement is a little different. Since the feet are anchored on the ground, the hip movement does not create translational movement until the regular kicking action starts. So the rotational movement of the hip creates the translational movement of the knee in the action of kicking. Rotational movement of the knee creates the translational movement of the ankle. The combination of the hip and the knee movement takes the ankle joint to the time and place to perform the lower-extremity actions. This stepwise rotational and translational enhancement is the most efficient mechanism in all the kinetic systems. It provides the speed and power in the athletic system. The whole body is operated under a seamless neurological control. It produces unified action at all times.

27

Following Through in Tennis, Golf Swing, and Kicking Motion

In tennis strokes or golf swings, we often hear the coaches ask their students to follow through. Obviously, in teaching the game of tennis and golf, there is problem of following through. What is following through anyway? I think we all know that this must be related to the racket and club swing. We also all understand that when we do something, we have to finish it and do not leave it partially undone. Nobody likes to leave something undone or not finish what he/she is supposed to do. There must be something that interferes with him/her. These kinds of interferences could be mental or physical. They could present a serious initial problem in learning during the initial stage and affect the player's performance during the performance stage. Now let's discuss in more detail.

A. Follow-Through Problems in Tennis Swing

When a tennis player uses his/her racket to strike at a tennis ball, there is a tendency that his/her racket will slow down or stop too early. Then the coach will say "follow through" and "follow through." Obviously, the coach is right.

If the coach gives a tennis racket with no string to the student and lets him/her hit a coming tennis ball, there will be no such problem. Or if the coach asks the student to close his eyes and make a swing as if he/she is hitting an incoming tennis ball, there will be no such problems either. Then we know that there is problem. There is something interfering with this student when he/she actually hitting a tennis ball.

From our biolink system, we know that the hip joint supports the upper body. The shoulder joint supports the elbow joint, and the elbow joint supports the wrist joint, and the wrist joint is the direct performing member. It is a sequential stepwise supporting system. Follow through is simply how other joints in the biolink chain actively work continuously following the wrist function. A short swing is a short following through. A full long swing is a full following through. This is a mental problem. It depends on the swing we are making. A well-controlled full swing in the mind will produce a complete following through. Our thought is on the execution of the swing we are making and not on the thought of the follow through, if we have the proper hitting concept to begin with.

Usually the problem of following through is caused by the player's eye moving or thinking about where the ball is going too early, and the swing is compromised.

B.   The Following Through in a Golf Swing

The golf swing and the tennis swing are a little different. During the tennis swing at the point of contact, the direction of acceleration of the racket is up. During the golf swing, at the point of contact, the direction of acceleration is down. Also, it is important that body weight distribution has to be fully behind the contact point since a golf swing is a well-planned total body rotation and a total rotational body motion is required.

It is important to know that if you let the shoulder turn within the turning path of the hip, let the elbow move within the path of the turning shoulder, and let the wrist move within the natural path of the total arm, then this will be a total integrated body turn for a consistent golf swing. This swing is most efficiently built on the basis of personal feeling. It is of the utmost importance in golf to build your own consistent swing.

The poor following through in golf is also caused by the early intention of seeing where the ball is going or just thinking about where the ball is going.

C. The Following Through in Kicking

Thinking of where the ball is going during the kicking action is also very common. With anything we do, if it is related to the distance, the throwing concept comes in. Since the throwing concept is so dominant in the human mind, it becomes the most detrimental interference factor intellectually. Our mind will think about where this flying object is going, and our eyes will simply follow what we think. The actions of hitting, throwing, and kicking have all been compromised. What we need is to be mentally tough, hit a hit, throw a throw, and kick a kick. If you just think about hitting and kicking when you are hitting and kicking, you will have enough time to finish your action completely.

28

Conclusion

This book is written based on the human system and simplified for people to understand on all levels. It is totally through personal soul-searching and intellectual reasoning. Most of the reasoning are predictions about the human system. Wishing all sport lovers would critically examine the contents and experiment with every fact mentioned. Any criticism will be sincerely welcomed.

Index

76057737R00102

Made in the USA
Lexington, KY
19 December 2017